Myrtle Ferguson

Jogging Through The Bible

DR. FRED LOWERY

Unless otherwise identified, scripture quotations are from the King James Version of the Bible.

Those who wish additional information on the teaching ministry of Dr. Fred Lowery are invited to write: **The First Word,** P.O. Box 6120, Bossier City, Louisiana 71171-6120.

A more detailed survey of the Bible is presented in **Walking Through the Bible,** by the same author.

REVISED EDITION
Library of Congress Catalog Card Number 83-051666
Copyright © 1982 by Titus Publishing Company
P.O. Box 6788 ● Corpus Christi, Texas 78411
All rights reserved
Printed in the United States of America

PREFACE

A few years ago, I began a study of the entire Bible using a book-by-book approach. As a result, my Sunday School class grew, my love for the Bible deepened, and finally a book emerged called "Walking Through The Bible."

In teaching the Bible, I discovered that people need some "handles" or "tools" to help them get a grip on the structure of God's Word and how it all comes together. I experimented with several different methods and then settled on using telephone numbers and key words. The phone numbers and key words became "joggables" to jog your memory concerning God's Word. My class loved the idea of having the phone numbers of Moses, David and Paul.

By memorizing <u>five</u> telephone numbers and <u>ten</u> words, anyone can get a grip on the structure and flow of the entire Bible. And, in addition, it's a whole lot of fun.

My friends who jog declare that it gets into their blood and becomes addictive. This book is intended to introduce you to spiritual jogging with the sincere hope that you find God's Word to be addictive.

Have fun!
Fred Lowery

To the congregation of
Pisgah Baptist Church of Spartanburg, South Carolina
and
First Baptist Church of Bossier City, Louisiana
whose enthusiastic response,
and transformed lives,
made the writing of this book
a must and a joy.

TABLE OF CONTENTS

Preface iii
Acknowledgments vi

Putting Yourself On a Program .. 1
Bible Reading Plan 2
A Word About the Joggables 4
Joggable One 5
   Getting Started 7
   The Bible's Movements
      and Subjects 8
Joggable Two 9
   Genesis 11
   Exodus 15
   Leviticus..................... 19
   Numbers 22
   Deuteronomy 25
Joggable Three................. 27
   Joshua 29
   Judges 32
   Ruth......................... 35
Joggable Four.................. 37
   I Samuel 39
   II Samuel 44
   I Kings....................... 45
   II Kings...................... 48
   I Chronicles.................. 50
   II Chronicles 52
Joggable Five 55
   Ezra 57
   Nehemiah 59
   Esther 61
Joggable Six 63
   Job.......................... 65
   Psalms 68
   Proverbs..................... 71
   Ecclesiastes.................. 73
   Song of Solomon............. 74
Joggable Seven 75
   Isaiah 77
   Jeremiah 80
   Lamentations................. 82
   Ezekiel 83
   Daniel 85
   Hosea 87
   Joel 89
   Amos........................ 91
   Obadiah 93
   Jonah 95

   Micah 97
   Nahum 98
   Habakkuk.................... 99
   Zephaniah 101
   Haggai 102
   Zechariah.................... 104
   Malachi...................... 106
Joggable Eight 109
Jogging Through The
      New Testament......... 117
Introducing the New Testament . 118
The Central Theme of the
      New Testament 119
Joggable Nine.................. 121
   The Subject of the Bible -
      Jesus Christ............. 123
   New Testament Authors 124
   A Brief Look at the
      Life of Christ 125
   The Gospels 127
   Matthew..................... 128
   Mark 130
   Luke......................... 132
   John......................... 134
   Acts......................... 136
   Romans 138
   I Corinthians................. 141
   II Corinthians 143
Joggable Ten................... 145
   Galatians.................... 147
   Ephesians 150
   Philippians 152
   Colossians 154
   I Thessalonians 156
   II Thessalonians 158
   I Timothy 161
   II Timothy.................... 163
   Titus 165
   Philemon 167
   Hebrews..................... 168
   James....................... 170
   I Peter 172
   II Peter 174
   I John 176
   II John....................... 178
   III John 180
   Jude......................... 182
   Revelation 184

ACKNOWLEDGMENTS

Special thanks to my secretaries, Janice Sharek and Vicky Long for typing this material. Also, thanks to Phyllis Ables for proofing the original manuscript and to Eddie Anders for the art work.

September 22, 1982
Pisgah Baptist Church
Spartanburg, S. C.

PUTTING YOURSELF ON A PROGRAM

1. Discipline (stickability) is the key to good spiritual health. There are no shortcuts.

2. Set aside a certain time each day for your spiritual jog. Let God speak to you through His Word and you speak to Him through prayer. An early morning jog is usually best, when the mind is fresh. If the morning doesn't suit, pick a time which fits your circumstances, but by all means keep your daily appointment with God.

3. As a warm up, read John 14:26 and recognize the presence of your instructor -- the Holy Spirit. Thank Him for His willingness to teach you all that you need to know.

4. Set your goal: to read the entire Bible in one year. For your convenience, we have included on the next page a plan whereby you can read through the entire Bible in one year.

5. Make a commitment to follow the Bible-reading plan.

6. Read slowly. It is good to read each chapter silently and then read it aloud.

7. Make it personal. Visualize yourself as the recipient of God's message. Each word is God speaking to man (you).

8. Read your class notes for additional help and information on the particular book(s) of the Bible you are studying. Add personal notes which will later jog your memory concerning what you have read.

9. Pray. Prayer is probably the greatest exercise one can ever perform. Spend some time talking to God as you would a very close friend. Be totally honest with Him.

" BUT EVERY ATHLETE GOES
INTO STRICT TRAINING."
I CORINTHIANS 9:25 (N.E.B.)

JANUARY

1	Genesis 1-2
2	Genesis 3-5
3	Genesis 6-9
4	Genesis 10-11
5	Genesis 12-14
6	Genesis 15-16
7	Genesis 17
8	Genesis 18-20
9	Genesis 21-23
10	Genesis 24-26
11	Genesis 27-31
12	Genesis 32-36
13	Genesis 37-38
14	Genesis 39-40
15	Genesis 41-44
16	Genesis 45-47
17	Genesis 48-50
18	Exodus 1-2
19	Exodus 3-6
20	Exodus 7-8
21	Exodus 9-10
22	Exodus 11-12
23	Exodus 13-15
24	Exodus 16-18
25	Exodus 19-20
26	Exodus 21-24
27	Exodus 25-26
28	Exodus 27-28
29	Exodus 29-31
30	Exodus 32-34
31	Exodus 35-40

FEBRUARY

1	Leviticus 1-3
2	Leviticus 4-7
3	Leviticus 8-9
4	Leviticus 10-11
5	Leviticus 12-15
6	Leviticus 16-20
7	Leviticus 21-23
8	Leviticus 24-27
9	Numbers 1-4
10	Numbers 5-6
11	Numbers 7-8
12	Numbers 9-12
13	Numbers 13-16
14	Numbers 17-20
15	Numbers 21-25
16	Numbers 26-30
17	Numbers 31-32
18	Numbers 33-34
19	Numbers 35-36
20	Deuteronomy 1-4
21	Deuteronomy 5-7
22	Deuteronomy 8-11
23	Deuteronomy 12-16
24	Deuteronomy 17-18
25	Deuteronomy 19-20
26	Deuteronomy 21-26
27	Deuteronomy 27-30
28	Deuteronomy 31-34

MARCH

1	Joshua 1-5
2	Joshua 6-8
3	Joshua 9-10
4	Joshua 11-12
5	Joshua 13-17
6	Joshua 18-21
7	Joshua 22-24
8	Judges 1-5
9	Judges 6-8
10	Judges 9-10
11	Judges 11-12
12	Judges 13-16
13	Judges 17-21
14	Ruth 1-4
15	1 Samuel 1-3
16	1 Samuel 4-8
17	1 Samuel 9-10
18	1 Samuel 11-12
19	1 Samuel 13-15
20	1 Samuel 16-19
21	1 Samuel 20-23
22	1 Samuel 24-26
23	1 Samuel 27-31
24	2 Samuel 1-2
25	2 Samuel 3-4
26	2 Samuel 5-7
27	2 Samuel 8-10
28	2 Samuel 11-14
29	2 Samuel 15-18
30	2 Samuel 19-20
31	2 Samuel 21-24

APRIL

1	1 Kings 1-4
2	1 Kings 5-8
3	1 Kings 9-11
4	1 Kings 12-16
5	1 Kings 17-19
6	1 Kings 20-22
7	2 Kings 1-2
8	2 Kings 3-4
9	2 Kings 5-8
10	2 Kings 9-12
11	2 Kings 13-17
12	2 Kings 18-21
13	2 Kings 22-25
14	1 Chronicles 1-5
15	1 Chronicles 6-9
16	1 Chronicles 10-16
17	1 Chronicles 17-21
18	1 Chronicles 22-27
19	1 Chronicles 28-29
20	2 Chronicles 1-5
21	2 Chronicles 6-7
22	2 Chronicles 8-9
23	2 Chronicles 10-12
24	2 Chronicles 13-16
25	2 Chronicles 17-20
26	2 Chronicles 21-25
27	2 Chronicles 26-28
28	2 Chronicles 29-30
29	2 Chronicles 31-32
30	2 Chronicles 33-36

MAY

1	Ezra 1-3
2	Ezra 4-6
3	Ezra 7-8
4	Ezra 9-10
5	Nehemiah 1-2
6	Nehemiah 3-4
7	Nehemiah 5-6
8	Nehemiah 7-8
9	Nehemiah 9-10
10	Nehemiah 11-13
11	Esther 1-2
12	Esther 3-4
13	Esther 5-6
14	Esther 7-8
15	Esther 9-10
16	Job 1-3
17	Job 4-7
18	Job 8-10
19	Job 11-12
20	Job 13-14
21	Job 15-17
22	Job 18-19
23	Job 20-21
24	Job 22-24
25	Job 25-28
26	Job 29-30
27	Job 31-32
28	Job 33-34
29	Job 35-37
30	Job 38-39
31	Job 40-42

JUNE

1	Psalms 1-6
2	Psalms 7-9
3	Psalms 10-12
4	Psalms 13-18
5	Psalms 19-24
6	Psalms 25-30
7	Psalms 31-36
8	Psalms 37-41
9	Psalms 42-44
10	Psalms 45-47
11	Psalms 48-53
12	Psalms 54-59
13	Psalms 60-66
14	Psalms 67-72
15	Psalms 73-77
16	Psalms 78-80
17	Psalms 81-82
18	Psalms 83-89
19	Psalms 90-97
20	Psalms 98-103
21	Psalms 104-106
22	Psalms 107-111
23	Psalms 112-115
24	Psalms 116-118
25	Psalms 119
26	Psalms 120-127
27	Psalms 128-135
28	Psalms 136-139
29	Psalms 140-144
30	Psalms 145-150

JULY

1 Proverbs 1-4
2 Proverbs 5-9
3 Proverbs 10-13
4 Proverbs 14-17
5 Proverbs 18-21
6 Proverbs 22-24
7 Proverbs 25-26
8 Proverbs 27-29
9 Proverbs 30-31
10 Ecclesiastes 1-6
11 Ecclesiastes 7-12
12 Song of Solomon 1-4
13 Song of Solomon 5-8
14 Isaiah 1-2
15 Isaiah 3-4
16 Isaiah 5-7
17 Isaiah 8-12
18 Isaiah 13-20
19 Isaiah 21-27
20 Isaiah 28-30
21 Isaiah 31-33
22 Isaiah 34-35
23 Isaiah 36-39
24 Isaiah 40-42
25 Isaiah 43-45
26 Isaiah 46-48
27 Isaiah 49-52
28 Isaiah 53-55
29 Isaiah 56-57
30 Isaiah 58-62
31 Isaiah 63-66

AUGUST

1 Jeremiah 1-6
2 Jeremiah 7-10
3 Jeremiah 11-15
4 Jeremiah 16-19
5 Jeremiah 19-20
6 Jeremiah 21-25
7 Jeremiah 26-29
8 Jeremiah 30-33
9 Jeremiah 34-36
10 Jeremiah 37-39
11 Jeremiah 40-42
12 Jeremiah 43-45
13 Jeremiah 46-52
14 Lamentations 1-5
15 Ezekiel 1-6
16 Ezekiel 7-11
17 Ezekiel 12-15
18 Ezekiel 16-17
19 Ezekiel 18-19
20 Ezekiel 20-24
21 Ezekiel 25-28
22 Ezekiel 29-32
23 Ezekiel 33-36
24 Ezekiel 37-39
25 Ezekiel 40-41
26 Ezekiel 42-43
27 Ezekiel 44-48
28 Daniel 1-3
29 Daniel 4-6
30 Daniel 7-9
31 Daniel 10-12

SEPTEMBER

1 Hosea 1-2
2 Hosea 3-4
3 Hosea 5-6
4 Hosea 7-8
5 Hosea 9-11
6 Hosea 12-14
7 Joel 1-3
8 Amos 1-2
9 Amos 3-4
10 Amos 5-6
11 Amos 7-8
12 Amos 9
13 Obadiah
14 Jonah 1-4
15 Micah 1
16 Micah 2
17 Micah 3-5
18 Micah 6-7
19 Nahum 1-3
20 Habakkuk 1-3
21 Zephaniah 1-3
22 Haggai 1
23 Haggai 2
24 Zechariah 1-2
25 Zechariah 3-6
26 Zechariah 7-8
27 Zechariah 9-11
28 Zechariah 12-14
29 Malachi 1-2
30 Malachi 3-4

OCTOBER

1 Matthew 1-4
2 Matthew 5-7
3 Matthew 8-10
4 Matthew 11-13
5 Matthew 14-18
6 Matthew 19-21
7 Matthew 22-23
8 Matthew 24-25
9 Matthew 26-28
10 Mark 1-3
11 Mark 4-7
12 Mark 8-10
13 Mark 11-12
14 Mark 13-14
15 Mark 15-16
16 Luke 1-2
17 Luke 3-6
18 Luke 7-9
19 Luke 10-12
20 Luke 13-14
21 Luke 15-16
22 Luke 17-18
23 Luke 19-21
24 Luke 22-24
25 John 1-3
26 John 4-6
27 John 7-8
28 John 9-10
29 John 11-12
30 John 13-17
31 John 18-21

NOVEMBER

1 Acts 1-2
2 Acts 3-7
3 Acts 8-9
4 Acts 10-11
5 Acts 12-13
6 Acts 14-15
7 Acts 16-18
8 Acts 19-20
9 Acts 21-23
10 Acts 24-25
11 Acts 26
12 Acts 27-28
13 Romans 1-3
14 Romans 4-5
15 Romans 6-8
16 Romans 9-11
17 Romans 12-14
18 Romans 15-16
19 I Corinthians 1-6
20 I Corinthians 7-10
21 I Corinthians 11-14
22 I Corinthians 15-16
23 2 Corinthians 1-4
24 2 Corinthians 5-7
25 2 Corinthians 8-9
26 2 Corinthians 10-13
27 Galatians
28 Ephesians
29 Philippians
30 Colossians

DECEMBER

1 I Thessalonians
2 2 Thessalonians
3 I Timothy
4 2 Timothy
5 Titus
6 Philemon
7 Hebrews 1
8 Hebrews 2
9 Hebrews 3
10 Hebrews 4
11 Hebrews 5-7
12 Hebrews 8-10
13 Hebrews 11-13
14 James
15 I Peter
16 2 Peter
17 I John
18 2 John
19 3 John
20 Jude
21 Revelations 1-2
22 Revelations 3
23 Revelations 4
24 Revelations 5
25 Revelations 6-7
26 Revelations 8-9
27 Revelations 10-13
28 Revelations 14-16
29 Revelations 17-18
30 Revelations 19-20
31 Revelations 21-22

A WORD ABOUT THE JOGGABLES

We have included ten joggables, or memory aids, to jog your memory and to enable you to recall those biblical facts stored in your personal computer – the brain.

By memorizing a handful of telephone numbers, one can have an excellent grasp of what the Bible is all about and the order in which things happened. We have included five telephone numbers for you to memorize.

The joggables are easily identified by the tennis shoe in the lower right hand corner.

<u>EXAMPLE</u>: Moses' phone number is 536-3517.

  5 = The five books of law
  3 = The Conquest of Canaan
  6 = The Kings and the Kingdoms
  3 = The Return and Restoration
  5 = The poets
  17 = The prophets

"FOR MY PART, I RUN WITH A CLEAR GOAL BEFORE ME."
         I CORINTHIANS 9:26 (N.E.B.)

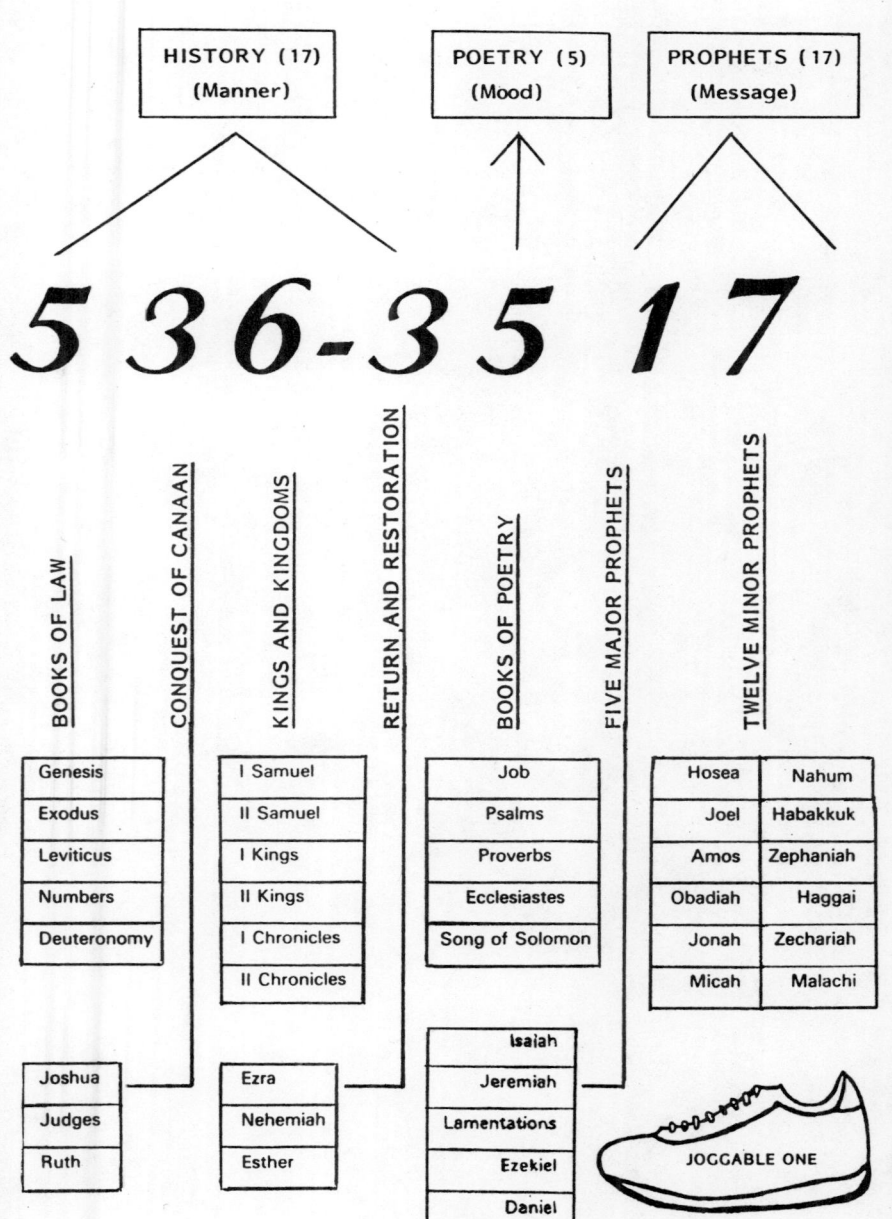

GETTING STARTED

Let's begin by looking over our Runner's Manual (the Bible) and see how we got this great book and what it's all about.

It Is the Inspired Word of God: II Timothy 3:16-17

Its Central Theme: Jesus Christ

Its Central Message: Salvation

Its Author: God, but He used ordinary men (40) over a period of 1600 years as His instruments to write down His mighty acts and words.

Its Language: The original writers wrote in Hebrew and Greek, but the Bible was translated into English by John Wycliffe in 1332 and our King James Version came along in 1611.

Its Divisions: Our Bible is divided into two major sections: the Old Testament with 39 separate books and the New Testament with 27 separate books for a total of 66 books -- all telling one story.

"YOUR SPIRITUAL LIFE LITERALLY DEPENDS ON EXERCISE. SO DON'T DREAD IT! LEARN TO LOVE IT!"

THE BIBLE HAS TWO GREAT MOVEMENTS

1. HUMAN HISTORY
2. DIVINE GOVERNMENT

THE BIBLE HAS THREE GREAT SUBJECTS

1. CREATION
2. THE LAW
3. THE SON OF GOD

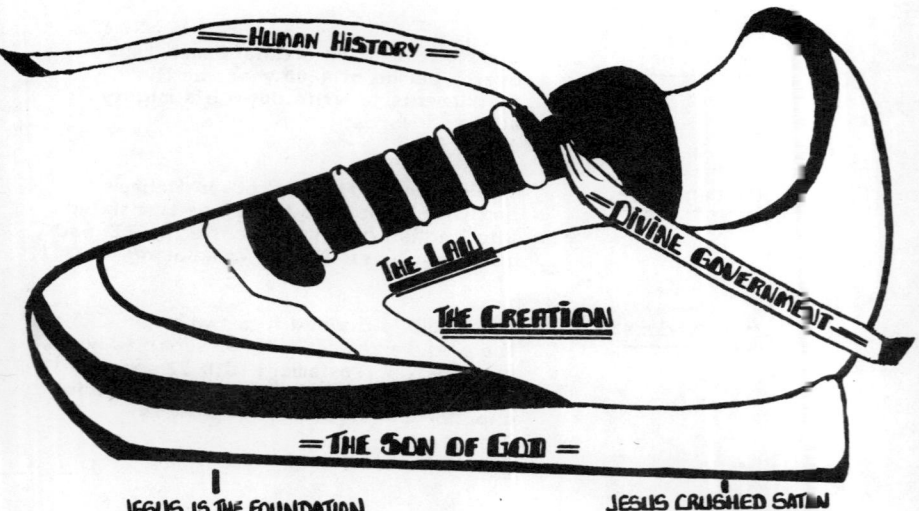

REMEMBER: THE LAW DID NOT FREE MAN — IT TIED (LACED) HIM UP ONLY THROUGH JESUS, THE SON OF GOD, IS MAN SET FREE.

"I PRESS TOWARDS THE GOAL TO WIN THE PRIZE WHICH IS GOD'S CALL TO THE LIFE ABOVE IN CHRIST JESUS."

PHILIPPIANS 3:14 (N.E.B.)

JOGGABLE TWO

THE FIRST FIVE BOOKS OF THE OLD TESTAMENT

(Law)

BOOK	KEY WORD	KEY PHRASE
GENESIS	"BEGINNING"	BEGINNING OF THE PEOPLE OF GOD
EXODUS	"LEAVING"	LEAVING EGYPT AND RECEIVING THE LAW
LEVITICUS	"LEARNING"	LEARNING HOW TO WORSHIP GOD
NUMBERS	"WANDERING"	WANDERING IN THE WILDERNESS
DEUTERONOMY	"REVIEWING"	REVIEWING GOD'S LAW

WORD OUTLINES

GENESIS	CREATION	CURSE	CALL
EXODUS	EGYPT	LAW	TABERNACLE
LEVITICUS	SACRIFICES	FEASTS	PRIESTHOOD
NUMBERS	WANDERING	MURMURING	RECEIVING
DEUTERONOMY	REVIEWING	RESTATING	RENEWING

TEN NAMES TO REMEMBER

1. GOD
2. ADAM
3. SATAN
4. NOAH
5. ABRAHAM
6. ISAAC
7. JACOB
8. JOSEPH
9. MOSES
10. JOSHUA

JOGGABLE TWO

JOGGING THROUGH GENESIS
(Roots, Beginnings)

JOGGING NOTES

I. **FACTS TO KNOW**

   A. <u>WRITER</u>: Moses

   B. <u>KEY VERSES</u>: Genesis 12:1-3

   C. <u>DATE</u>: Creation to about 2000 - 2400 B.C.

   D. <u>PURPOSE</u>: A religious history showing:

       1. Man and his sin
       2. God and His salvation

   E. <u>THEME</u>: The saving acts of God

II. **FOOD TO GROW**

   A. <u>GENESIS IS</u>:

     1. <u>A Book of Beginnings</u>

        Beginning of all things except God:

           World, man, sabbath, marriage, sin, prophecy, sacrifice, nations, Israel, etc.

     2. A Book of Foundation

        a. <u>For the Bible</u>

           Introduces the Bible
           Seed plot to the Word of God
           Presents principles of God's relationship with man
           Identifies sin and pictures salvation
           Relates an eternal covenant (promise)
           Exposes Satan as enemy of God and deceiver of man
           Reveals the chosen family of God

        b. <u>For Theology</u>

           "In the beginning God..." (Genesis 1:1)

              Behind all things, before all things
              Above all things, in all things

     3. <u>A Book of Eternal Promises</u>

        a. <u>To Satan</u>: Genesis 3

(1) His ultimate destruction
(2) His eternal doom

    b. To the Chosen People of God:

       (1) They would inherit the land of Canaan
       (2) They would become a great nation
       (3) They would become God's instrument to bless the world.

    The above promises were first given to Abraham (12:1-3) and then repeated to Isaac and Jacob (26:1-5; 28:13-15)

    c. To All Men: Genesis 3:15

       (1) Good will ultimately win and evil will lose
       (2) Jesus, seed of woman, will defeat Satan at Calvary
       (3) Promise fulfilled in John 3:16

4. A Book of Consistent Failure

Genesis, as well as the entire Bible, presents a picture of man's failure -- but also of God meeting man at the point of failure. Man failed in Eden's ideal garden, then under the rule of conscience, and finally under patriarchal rule. So Genesis gives us at least 2000 years of failing, sinning man being brought to a God of love and grace.

B. GENESIS TELLS ABOUT:

1. The Forming

God created the heavens and the earth and everything within them. He created man in His own image (spiritual likeness) and gave him dominion over all the earth.

2. The Fall

Satan, acting through a serpent, tempted man to doubt God's Word, His authority, and goodness. As a result, man failed his test to freely serve God and wanted to be God himself. Man's fall resulted in shame and separation from God. The penalty of sin was a curse upon the ground and upon nature, as well as sorrow in the heart.

3. The Flood

Because of man's exceeding wickedness, God would send a flood to destroy the world. God found one righteous man, Noah, and instructed him to build an ark. The flood came and the waters covered the earth and only Noah, his three sons, their wives, and all the animals were saved.

4. The Floundering (Tower of Babel)

Following the flood, the world was given a new start, but again disobeyed God. They were commanded to scatter out and repeople the earth, but in defiance of God built a city and the famous Tower of Babel. Because of pride, the people wanted to be independent of God and protected from God. Therefore, God, in judgment for this, confused their tongues and forced them to scatter. The nations were then divided according to the three sons of Noah -- Shem, Ham, and Japheth. (See Genesis 10 and 11)

5. The Founding Fathers (Abraham, Isaac, Jacob, Joseph)

Out of all the people of the earth, God chose a man named Abraham to be the father of a mighty nation and to begin the history of God's chosen people Israel. God wanted a chosen people for at least three reasons:

a. To Have a Prepared People to Whom He Could Entrust the Scriptures

b. To Have a Channel Through Whom the Promised Messiah Would Come

c. To Have a Witness to the Other Nations

God made a covenant with Abraham and repeated the covenant to Abraham's son, Isaac, and again to his grandson, Jacob. God permitted Jacob's son, Joseph, to be sold into Egypt, and Jacob's family to follow him there in order to be protected from a great famine. Jacob's (name changed to Israel) 12 sons became the heads of the 12 tribes of Israel.

A large portion of Genesis is devoted to Joseph (37-48) as the link between a family and the nation. The people go into Egypt as a small family of 70 people but come out (Exodus) as a large nation of more than two million people.

JOGGING NOTES

JOGGING RECORD SHEET
(Genesis)

THE BEGINNINGS OF THE WORLD (Chapters 1 - 11)	THE BEGINNINGS OF ISRAEL (Chapters 12 - 50)
1. The Forming, Chapters 1 - 2	1. Abraham, Chapters 12 - 23
2. The Fall, Chapters 3 - 5	2. Isaac, Chapters 24 - 26
3. The Flood, Chapters 6 - 9	3. Jacob, Chapters 27 - 36
4. The Floundering, Chapters 10-11	4. Joseph, Chapters 37 - 50

#			#		
1			26		
2			27		
3			28		
4			29		
5			30		
6			31		
7			32		
8			33		
9			34		
10			35		
11			36		
12			37		
13			38		
14			39		
15			40		
16			41		
17			42		
18			43		
19			44		
20			45		
21			46		
22			47		
23			48		
24			49		
25			50		

JOGGING THROUGH EXODUS

I. **FACTS TO KNOW**

   A. **TITLE:** Exodus means "way out" (exit)

   B. **WRITER AND MAIN CHARACTER:** Moses

   C. **THEME:** Redemption of God's people

   D. **KEY VERSE:** Exodus 3:8

   E. **DATE:** Around 1400 B.C.

   F. **PURPOSE:** To continue the story of Genesis -- beginning with Israel in Egyptian bondage, tracing the events of their deliverance and ending with the establishment of the law and the erecting of the tabernacle.

II. **FOOD TO GROW**

   A. **EXODUS PICTURES SALVATION**

      1. **A Type of Deliverance**

         The story of Exodus is repeated in the life of every person seeking true deliverance. Christ, on the cross, is our Passover Lamb and delivers us from the bondage of our sins just as Israel was delivered from the bondage of Egypt. As the Exodus under Moses meant new life, liberty, and fellowship - salvation through Christ means all this and more to the believer.

      2. **A Type of All True Redemption**

         It was accomplished wholly through the power of God, by means of a deliverer, and under the cover of blood.

   B. **EXODUS TELLS ABOUT:**

      1. **Bondage**

         Following the death of Joseph, a new king arose in Egypt who severely oppressed the Israelites. The people of God were treated as slaves and forced to do hard labor under the cruel Egyptian taskmasters. Finally, an attempt was made to destroy all the male children and thereby destroy the seed of Abraham, preventing the coming of the promised Messiah.

      2. **Moses**

         Moses wrote Genesis with pre-existing documents but Exodus begins the story of Moses: his birth,

JOGGING NOTES

call, and ministry as God's leader, deliverer, and lawgiver of Israel. It is interesting that while Satan was using Pharaoh to destroy Israel, God was using Pharaoh's daughter to raise up a deliverer. Moses prepared for his ministry in the desert, received his call at the burning bush near Sinai, and led God's people out of Egypt and to the edge of the Promised Land of Canaan.

3. Plagues

Moses, following the will of God, confronted the Pharaoh of Egypt with a message from God: "Let my people go!" Pharaoh, with a hardened heart, refused to let God's people go and God sent 10 plagues upon him - each one increasing in severity.

4. The Passover

On a certain night, as a part of the tenth and final plague, God's angel would pass over and destroy the eldest child in every Egyptian home. For protection, the Hebrew families were instructed to kill a lamb and sprinkle its blood upon the door post, thereby saving their children from death. Through the centuries, the Hebrews have kept the Passover as a commemorative feast to remind them of their deliverance from Egypt. The Passover is a striking picture of the greatest deliverance accomplished by Christ on the cross.

5. The Law

God's people, now numbering between two and three million, are out of Egypt and on their journey to the Promised Land. Israel is assembled in the wilderness at Sinai to worship God and to receive the law. The law is divided into three parts: (1) the moral law - Ten Commandments, (2) the ceremonial law, (3) the civil law. The purpose of the law is twofold: (1) to provide God's standard of holiness and (2) to show man's sinfulness.

6. The Tabernacle

Instructions were given at Sinai for the building of a portable sanctuary, known as the tabernacle -- the place where God meets His people. The exact pattern was given to Moses and the scriptures devote more room to the description of the tabernacle than to any other subject. In the New Testament, Jesus becomes our tabernacle.

C. <u>EXODUS RECORDS</u>

The three great foundational events of the Old Testament:

1. The Deliverance from Egypt – Passover
2. The Giving of the Law at Sinai
3. The Erection of the Tabernacle in the Wilderness

JOGGING NOTES

JOGGING RECORD SHEET
(Exodus)

GOD REDEEMING HIS PEOPLE FROM THEIR ENEMIES		

LEAVING:
     I. The Exit, Chapters 1 – 18
    II. The Law, Chapters 19 – 24
    III. The Tabernacle, Chapters 25 – 40		

GOD GIVING THE LAW AND TEACHING HIS PEOPLE HOW TO LIVE		
1	21	
2	22	
3	23	
4	24	
5	25	
6	26	
7	27	
8	28	
9	29	
10	30	
11	31	
12	32	
13	33	
14	34	
15	35	
16	36	
17	37	
18	38	
19	39	
20	40	

JOGGING THROUGH LEVITICUS

JOGGING NOTES

I. **FACTS TO KNOW**

   A. <u>TITLE</u>: Leviticus gets its name from Levi (Levites) one of the twelve tribes set aside by God to serve as priests (mediators) between God and the Hebrew nation in the ministry of animal sacrifices.

   B. <u>WRITER</u>: Moses

   C. <u>THEME</u>: "Man's holy walk with a holy God." Fellowship with God is based on a cleansed life and a holy walk.

   D. <u>DATE</u>: About 1439 B.C., a little over a year after leaving Egypt.

   E. <u>OUTSTANDING CHARACTER</u>: Aaron, the high priest and a type of Christ

   F. <u>KEY WORD</u>: Holiness (87 times)

   G. <u>PURPOSE</u>: God's people are still at Sinai and are being taught the proper way to worship God. They are receiving instructions concerning the different <u>sacrifices</u> and <u>offerings</u>, along with the necessary priestly functions. God is speaking to man through the tabernacle and showing that the way to God is through sacrifice, and the walk with God is by separation.

II. **FOOD TO GROW**

   A. <u>LEVITICUS TELLS ABOUT</u>:

     1. The Offerings (Sacrifices) *1-7*

       God has made provision for His people (sinful man) to approach Him (Holy God) in worship. Since there can be no fellowship with God until sin has been dealt with -- the only way is through sacrifice (offerings). These sacrifices did not in themselves satisfy God, but were object lessons pointing to the person and the sacrifice of the Lord Jesus Christ. (See John 1:29)

     2. The Priesthood *ch. 8-10*

       Since no one was permitted to bring his own offering to God, it was necessary for a priest

JOGGING NOTES

to stand between God and man. Sacrifice was the basis and the priesthood was the means of access to God. Out of the 12 tribes, God chose the tribe of Levi to be the priestly tribe -- called Levites. Aaron, the high priest, and his sons were in charge of the sacrifices and all other Levites were assistants to the priests and took care of the tabernacle. They were teachers, scribes, musicians, officers, and were supported by tithes and offerings of the other 11 tribes.

3. **The Feasts** *ch. 11-15*

There are eight feasts described in the last section of Leviticus which serve as reminders and provisions for holy living.

4. **The Day of Atonement** *ch. 16-17*

On this day the sins of the nation were confessed and Jehovah's relationship to His people was established. Only the high priest could enter the Holy of Holies and sprinkle blood on the mercy seat on behalf of the nation.

ch. 18 - Walk with God

JOGGING RECORD SHEET
(Leviticus)

MAN LEARNING HOW TO WORSHIP AND WALK WITH GOD	
I. Sacrifices II. Feasts III. Priesthood	

	THE WAY TO GOD SACRIFICE		THE WALK WITH GOD SEPARATION
1		15	
2		16	
3		17	
4		18	
5		19	
6		20	
7		21	
8		22	
9		23	
10		24	
11		25	
12		26	
13		27	
14			

JOGGING THROUGH NUMBERS
(Wilderness Wandering)

God's people are "in the wilderness" spending 40 years on a 40 day journey.

I. **FACTS TO KNOW**

   A. <u>TITLE</u>: Numbers is used because the book records the two numberings of the Israelites – before leaving Sinai and before entering Canaan.

   B. <u>WRITER</u>: Moses

   C. <u>THEME</u>: The discipline of God's people.

   D. <u>KEY VERSES</u>: Numbers 1:1-2

   E. <u>KEY WORD</u>: Wilderness (45 times)

   F. <u>PURPOSE</u>: To give a historical record of the 40 years of wilderness wanderings of Israel brought on by their unbelief and to record the census of the two generations.

II. **FOOD TO GROW**

   A. <u>NUMBERS EMPHASIZES DISCIPLINE</u>

     1. The Law Had Been Given.

     2. The Tabernacle Had Been Built.

     3. The Priests Had Been Assigned Their Service.

     4. Now, God Prepares the Nation For Its Work.

   B. <u>NUMBERS TELLS ABOUT</u>:

     1. God's Promises

       Here we find proof that God's presence provides everything. We have three million people on a sterile desert, without a drop of water or any visible means of support, and yet God provides for their needs. Even their shoes lasted 40 years and didn't wear out.

     2. Murmuring

       The spirit of discontent and unbelief showed itself in the form of murmuring. God's people

---

JOGGING NOTES

1-4 vs. counted
603,550
5-10 vs. counselled
nazarites vow
11-12 vs. chastised
70 elders
13-14 vs. condemned
Joshua
Caleb
said could do it.
15-20 vs. wilderness
new generation
21-36 vs.

lusted for the things of Egypt, criticized their leaders, disobeyed God, and refused to go forward.

JOGGING NOTES

3. Joshua and Caleb

Moses, at God's command, sent 12 men out as spies and after 40 days they returned with a discouraging report. However, two men -- Joshua and Caleb -- wanted to obey God and move forward, but the people turned back. Therefore, God allowed only Joshua and Caleb to enter Canaan. All others would die in the wilderness.

4. Moses' Successor

Moses was warned of his approaching death and asked the Lord to appoint a man over the people. He was instructed to ordain Joshua as his successor.

C. THE OUTSTANDING CHARACTERS:

1. Moses - the Great Leader

2. Aaron - the High Priest and Moses' Brother

3. Miriam - the Sister of Moses and Aaron

4. Joshua - a Spy Who Dared to Believe God

5. Caleb - a Spy Who Dared to Believe God

D. SOME IMPORTANT LESSONS

1. God Loves Order and Design

2. God Has a Job for Everyone

3. The Seriousness of Sin

4. The Impossibility of Hiding Sin

5. God is Concerned With the Daily Details of Life

6. Following and Obeying God is the Key to Happiness

JOGGING RECORD SHEET
(Numbers)

JOURNEYING FROM SINAI TO BORDER OF CANAAN (About 40 Years)			

IN THE WILDERNESS:
              I. Wandering
             II. Murmuring
           III. Receiving			

SPENDING 40 YEARS ON A 40 DAY TRIP – THE RESULT OF DISOBEDIENCE			
1		19	
2		20	
3		21	
4		22	
5		23	
6		24	
7		25	
8		26	
9		27	
10		28	
11		29	
12		30	
13		31	
14		32	
15		33	
16		34	
17		35	
18		36	

JOGGING THROUGH DEUTERONOMY

JOGGING NOTES

I. FACTS TO KNOW

A. **TITLE:** Deuteronomy means "second law," but it is really a restating and further exposition of the law to the new generation.

B. **WRITER:** Moses

C. **THEME:** To love and obey God is the way of happiness and blessing.

D. **DATE:** About 1400 B.C., covering a time span of two months.

E. **KEY WORD:** Obedience

F. **KEY VERSE:** Deuteronomy 6:5

G. **PURPOSE:** Moses, God's great leader is about to die and is trying to prepare God's people for their entrance, conquest, and possession of Canaan.

14 times quoted in New Testament

Yahweh Jehovah is our God

II. FOOD TO GROW

A. **DEUTERONOMY TELLS ABOUT:**

1. **Moses Reviewing the Past**

   We have a series of messages from Moses to Israel at the end of their long wilderness journey. He reminds them of God's past goodness and of the importance of their obedience to God's way and Word.

   Chs. 1-4

2. **Moses Restating the Law**

   Moses restates the law that was given on Mt. Sinai and then gives an extended exposition and application of it.   *Exodus 20*

   Chs. 5-26
   6-21 10 commandments

3. **Moses Renewing the Covenant**

   As long as the people were faithful to God, they would remain in Canaan and prosper; but should they be unfaithful, God would bring judgment on them and terminate their stay and their prosperity.

   Chs. 27-30

4. **Moses Reaching the End**

   The closing chapters record Moses' final messages to Israel along with the closing events of his life. The great lawgiver of Israel dies and the books of law come to an end.

   Chs. 31-34
   Moses dies

JOGGING RECORD SHEET

(Deuteronomy)

REMEMBER WHAT GOD HAS SAID

Moses:
    I. Reviewing the Past, Chapters 1 - 4
   II. Restating the Law, Chapters 5 - 26
  III. Renewing the Covenant, Chapters 27 - 30
  IV. Reaching the End, Chapters 31 - 34

#		#		
1		18		
2		19		
3		20		
4		21		
5		22		
6		23		
7		24		
8		25		
9		26		
10		27		
11		28		
12		29		
13		30		
14		31		
15		32		
16		33		
17		34		

JOGGABLE THREE
LET'S JOG THROUGH THE CONQUEST OF CANAAN

BOOK	KEY WORD	KEY PHRASE
JOSHUA	"CONQUERING"	CONQUERING THE LAND OF CANAAN
JUDGES	"JUDGING"	JUDGING THE SINS OF THE PEOPLE
RUTH	"LOVING"	LOVING THE TRUE GOD OF ISRAEL

WORD OUTLINES

JOSHUA	ENTERING	CONQUERING	DIVIDING
JUDGES	DISOBEDIENCE	DEFEAT	DELIVERANCE
RUTH	CHOICE	PATIENCE	REWARD

REVIEW

BOOK	KEY WORD	KEY PHRASE
GENESIS	"BEGINNING"	BEGINNING OF THE PEOPLE OF GOD
EXODUS	"LEAVING"	LEAVING EGYPT AND RECEIVING THE LAW
LEVITICUS	"LEARNING"	LEARNING HOW TO WORSHIP GOD
NUMBERS	"WANDERING"	WANDERING IN THE WILDERNESS
DEUTERONOMY	"REVIEWING"	REVIEWING GOD'S LAW
JOSHUA	"CONQUERING"	CONQUERING THE LAND OF CANAAN
JUDGES	"JUDGING"	JUDGING THE SINS OF THE PEOPLE
RUTH	"LOVING"	LOVING THE TRUE GOD OF ISRAEL

JOGGABLE THREE

JOGGING THROUGH JOSHUA (author)

JOGGING NOTES

I. FACTS TO KNOW

A. TITLE: Joshua means "God's Salvation" and the New Testament makes it clear that Joshua is a type of Christ.

✓

B. WRITER: Joshua

C. KEY VERSE: Joshua 1:2-3

D. KEY WORDS: Possession
Inheritance

E. THEME: The conquest and settlement of the children of Israel in the Promised Land (Canaan). It was Joshua, not Moses (representing the law), who brought Israel into Canaan.

25 to 30 yr. period

F. PURPOSE: To record the conquest and allocation of the land and to reaffirm the faithfulness and presence of God.

II. FOOD TO GROW

A. JOSHUA TELLS ABOUT:

1. **Entering the Land**

   Joshua sent two spies to the key city of Jericho and the spies were received and protected by Rahab. *prostitute* Guided now, not by a pillar of fire, but by the Ark (God's presence), Israel prepares to cross the Jordan and enter the Promised Land.

   1-5 entering the land.

2. **Crossing the Jordan**

   The crossing of Jordan, like the Red Sea, was a momentous crisis in the history of Israel. To cross Jordan was to become committed, without the possibility of retreat, to face the giants of Canaan. *achan*

   6-12 - conquering the land.

3. **The Renewal of Circumcision and the Passover**

   That which had been neglected during the 40 years of wandering in unbelief, now becomes imperative. Circumcision is the seal of the covenant between God and Israel.

   13-24 dividing the land.

4. Conquering the Land

God had promised Canaan to His people, but there were battles to be fought and the enemy to be driven out. As is true in the Christian life, God promises victory, but He doesn't fight our battles for us. Jericho, the first city in Canaan, was conquered, then Ai, and then on to possess the land.

5. Dividing the Land

The last half of the book (13 - 24) deals with the division of Canaan according to the tribes. The method was by "casting lots before the Lord."

6. The Farewell of Joshua

The last two chapters record the closing events in the life of Joshua, who died at the age of 110.

B. JOSHUA REPRESENTS THREE STAGES OF THE SPIRITUAL LIFE

EGYPT	THE WILDERNESS	CANAAN
The World	The Defeated Christian Life	The Victorious Life
"Unbelief"	"Carnality"	"Faith"

JOGGING NOTES

JOGGING RECORD SHEET
(Joshua)

VICTORY: WHAT GOD GIVES IS OURS TO POSSESS

    I.   Entering the Land, Chapters 1 - 5
   II.   Conquering the Land, Chapters 6 - 12
  III. Dividing the Land, Chapters 13 - 24

The Call to Joshua (1)
The Mission of the Spies (2)
The Jordan Crossed (3)
The Memorial Stones (4)
The Renewal of Circumcision
  and Passover (5)
The Fall of Jericho (6)
The Sin of Achan (7)

The Defeat of Ai (8)
The Deceit of Gideon (9)
The General Conquest (10 - 12)
The Division of Canaan (13 - 19)
The Cities of Refuge (20)
The Cities of the Levites (21)
The Two-and-a-half Tribes (22)
The Farewell of Joshua (23 - 24)

#		#	
1		13	
2		14	
3		15	
4		16	
5		17	
6		18	
7		19	
8		20	
9		21	
10		22	
11		23	
12		24	

JOGGING THROUGH JUDGES
(The Dark Ages)

Israel had no king and so "every man did what was right in his own eyes."

I. **FACTS TO KNOW**

    A. <u>WRITER</u>: Uncertain, probably Samuel or one of his associates.

    B. <u>THEME</u>: The theme is twofold: the frequent backslidings of Israel and the constant grace of God.

    C. <u>PURPOSE</u>: To give a historical account of the activities of the twelve judges (15 including Abimelech, Samuel, and Eli) who ruled from the death of Joshua to the coronation of King Saul (about 300 years.)

    D. <u>KEY VERSE</u>: Judges 21:25

    E. <u>KEY WORD</u>: Judgment

    F. <u>DATE</u>: About 1400 - 1100 B.C.

II. **FOOD TO GROW**

    A. <u>JUDGES TELLS ABOUT</u>:

        1. The Judges

        The Israelite people forsake God, <u>and</u>, in their disobedience, gave themselves over to idolatry and immorality. As a means of discipline, God forsakes them and leaves them in the hands of their cruel enemies. In desperation, they cry out to the Lord for help, and He delivers them by raising up a "judge" to lead them to victory. The judges first delivered the people and then ruled over them.

        2. The Pattern of Israel's Backslidings (Sins)

        Once the people of God are delivered and begin to enjoy peace and prosperity, they turn again and forsake their Lord. This pattern is repeated throughout the book.

JOGGING NOTES

The pattern: (repeated seven times in the book)

    Israel's disobedience to God's rule
    Oppression by warring neighbors
    Deliverance by the judges

3. Israel's Oppression and Deliverance

The heart of the book (chapters 3 - 16) gives us the picture of Israel's seven failures, seven oppressions from their warring neighbors, and seven deliverances.

4. Israel's Corruption

The last chapters (17-21) present a picture of anarchy and confusion. There is corruption in the religious, moral, and political life of Israel.

B. THE OUTSTANDING CHARACTERS

1. Deborah (the only woman judge) was a great mother and a remarkable person whom God raised up to deliver Israel from Jabin, King of Canaan. Deborah took the lead when no man would.

2. Gideon was raised up at a time of national emergency to become the most important of all the judges in history. His recruited army of 32,000 was whittled down to a pitiful 300, and then given no weapons. Yet, there has never been a greater victory in all of history.

3. Samson had a golden opportunity to deliver Israel but ends up as one of the most colossal failures in scripture.

4. The other judges: Othniel, Ehud, Shamgar, Barak, Tola, Jair, Jephthah, Ibzan, Elon, and Abdon. Also, Samuel (prophet-judge), Eli (priest judge), and Ablimelech, who was not called of God to judge.

JOGGING RECORD SHEET
(Judges)

THE DARK DAYS OF ISRAEL'S HISTORY	
I. Disobedience II. Defeat III. Deliverance	
1	12
2	13
3	14
4	15
5	16
6	17
7	18
8	19
9	20
10	21
11	22

JOGGING THROUGH RUTH
(Other side of Dark Ages)

During the dark and chaotic period of the judges, the beautiful story of Ruth is as a rose in a desert.

I. **FACTS TO KNOW**

   A. TITLE: The name is taken from Ruth, the principle character. Only two books in the Bible bear the name of a woman (Ruth and Esther).

   B. WRITER: Unknown, possibly Samuel.

   C. DATE: The story took place in the period of the judges, but the writing came after David had become king (4:17,22)

   D. THEME: A story of faith and love where Ruth, an "outsider," chooses to serve the Lord God of Israel with her whole heart and through God's grace is exalted to a high place of privilege and honor (2:12).

   E. PURPOSE: To give a historical account of the brighter side of life during the period of the judges, tracing the ancestry of David, and showing that divine blessing is on the one who serves God.

   F. KEY VERSES: Ruth 1:16-17

   G. KEY WORDS: kinsman, redeem

II. **FOOD TO GROW**

   A. RUTH TELLS ABOUT:

   1. A Story of Love

      In those dark days when the judges ruled, a severe famine drove Elimelech and Naomi and their two sons from their home in Bethlehem, across the Jordan to the land of Moab. Soon their sons married Ruth and Orpah, women of Moab. Elimelech and his sons died, leaving all three women to widowhood. Naomi, in her loneliness, decided to return to her native land and bids her daughters-in-law a tender farewell. She urged them to return to their fathers' homes and Orpah did. Ruth, however, had be-

JOGGING NOTES

come a true worshipper of the true God and through her love for God and Naomi she would go with Naomi. Her reply to Naomi is one of the most beautiful passages in all God's Word and is recorded in Ruth 1:16. Naomi and Ruth go to live in Bethlehem where Ruth gleans in the wheat and barley fields of Boaz. Boaz falls in love with Ruth and marries her. To this marriage was born Obed, the grandfather of David.

JOGGING NOTES

2. A Story of Grace

Boaz was the son of Rahab, the Jericho harlot (Joshua 2:1; Matt. 1:5). That means that David can be traced through a Moabite and a Canaanite, demonstrating the grace of God. Ruth is the great-grandmother of David, the ancestor of Christ.

3. A Story of Redemption

Boaz is a picture of Christ, our kinsman-redeemer, who rescued us from our lost condition by fully paying the price for our sin. Boaz took Ruth (a Gentile woman) into the Davidic ancestry and Messianic line. As Ruth passes into that line, she representatively takes all the Gentiles with her.

B. THE MAIN CHARACTERS

1. Ruth
2. Naomi
3. Boaz

JOGGING RECORD SHEET
(Ruth)

A BEAUTIFUL LOVE STORY
Redeeming Love: 　　　　Its Choice 　　　　Its Patience 　　　　Its Reward

1	
2	
3	
4	

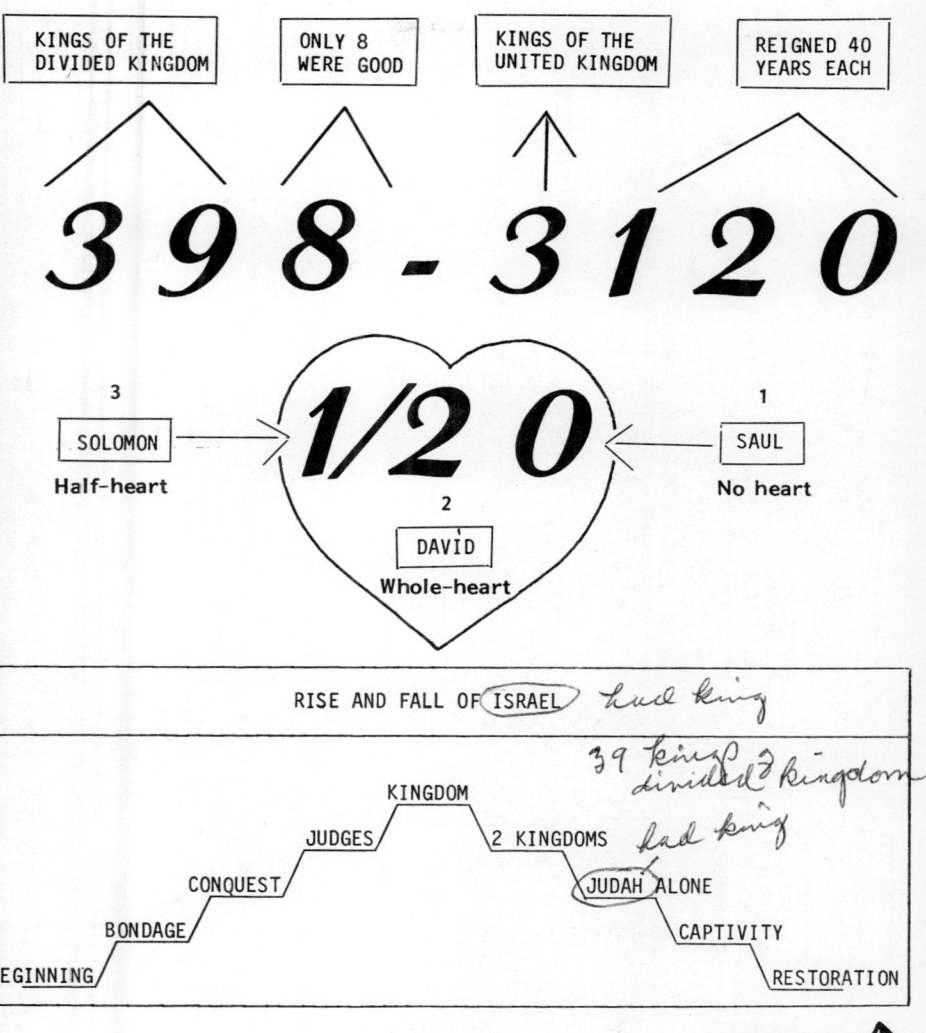

JOGGING THROUGH FIRST SAMUEL

JOGGING NOTES

The beginning of royal history; changing from a theocracy (God-rule) to a monarchy (man-rule).

I. **FACTS TO KNOW**

    A. **TITLE**: The book takes its name from Samuel, the last of the judges and the one who annointed Saul and David as Israel's first kings.

    B. **WRITER**: Unknown, but Jewish tradition accredited the book to Samuel (10:25).

    C. **KEY VERSE**: I Samuel 8:5

    D. **KEY WORD**: Prayer

    E. **DATE**: Between 1100 B.C. and 950 B.C., from the birth of Samuel (the last of the judges and the first of the prophets) to the death of Saul (the first of the kings), a period of about 100 years.

    F. **THEME**: The long period of the judges had left Israel rejecting God and begging for an earthly king. So, we view the nation in the difficult days of transition through the eyes of Samuel, Saul, and David.

        THREE GREAT MEN

        1. Samuel: The last of the judges
        2. Saul: The first of the kings
        3. David: The greatest of the kings

    G. **PURPOSE**: The book, historical in nature, traces the history of Israel from the birth of Samuel to the death of Saul.

II. **FOOD TO GROW**

    A. **FIRST SAMUEL TELLS ABOUT**:

        1. **Samuel** (Chapters 1-7)

        Samuel, in his influence on the early growth of the nation, is equaled only by Moses. He came upon the scene at a time when it seemed that hopeless Israel would be crushed and yet he stopped the nation's decay, established an orderly and progressive kingdom, and planted it on the path of greatness. Samuel, a man of prayer, was always God's man. The first seven chapters are given to the birth, childhood, call, and ministry of Samuel.

JOGGING NOTES

2. Saul (Chapters 8-15)

"I gave thee a king in mine anger, and took him away in my wrath" (Hosea 13:11) can be written over the remainder of First Samuel. God intended to be Israel's only king, but Israel refused to have it that way. They pestered God, criticized and complained, until God gave them their way. So, Saul becomes man's choice for king and was appointed and annointed as king over Israel. No man ever had a greater opportunity than Saul, and no man was ever a greater failure. His failure was in his self-will; he would not follow God.

3. David (Chapters 16-31)

While Saul was man's choice, David was God's choice. David was chosen on the basis of the heart, while Saul was chosen on the basis of outward appearance. The war with the Philistines gave David the opportunity to reveal the quality of his character as he went out to meet and defeat Goliath. Saul, because of David's great success, became insanely jealous and tried five times to kill David - but God spared his life. God uses the long period of David's trials, fleeing from Saul, to disciple him and prepare him to be Israel's greatest king.

B. THE RISE OF THE PROPHETS

Even though some have been called prophets, there was no organized prophetic office until Samuel. This man of God founded the "School of the Prophets" and originated the prophetic order. In a real sense, he was the first of the prophets. Now, the prophet becomes the messenger of God in place of the priest.

JOGGING RECORD SHEET
(First Samuel)

THE BEGINNING OF ROYAL HISTORY

I. Samuel – the Last of the Judges, Chapters 1 – 7
II. Saul – the First of the Kings, Chapters 8 – 15
III. David – the Greatest of the Kings, Chapters 16 – 31

1		17	
2		18	
3		19	
4		20	
5		21	
6		22	
7		23	
8		24	
9		25	
10		26	
11		27	
12		28	
13		29	
14		30	
15		31	
16			

JOGGING THROUGH SECOND SAMUEL

JOGGING NOTES

The reign of David, God's king, and Israel's greatest king.

I. FACTS TO KNOW

   A. WRITER: Uncertain, but tradition places Samuel responsible for the first 24 chapters of First Samuel. The remaining chapters, along with all of Second Samuel, are the work of two prophets - Nathan and Gad.

   B. THEME: The story of David, as King of Israel, and of the "House of David," through which the Messiah would later come.

   C. KEY VERSES: II Samuel 5:5, 7:16

   D. KEY WORD: David (280 times)

   E. DATE: Around 1000 B.C. - 961 B.C.

   F. PURPOSE: To record the history of Israel from Saul's death to the beginning of Solomon's reign.

FIRST SAMUEL: THE FAILURE OF MAN'S KING

SECOND SAMUEL: THE ENTHRONEMENT OF GOD'S KING

II. FOOD TO GROW

   A. SECOND SAMUEL TELLS ABOUT:

      1. David's Triumphs (Chapters 1-12)

         David stands as one of the most important characters in God's Word. He ranks with Abraham and Moses as one of the three most outstanding characters in the Old Testament. He is seen as the shepherd boy, the court musician, the loyal friend, the soldier and leader, the great general, the king, the loving father, the sinner, the broken-hearted father - but always the lover of God. David's religious experiences are given in the Psalms. He is the most complete picture of Christ in the Old

Testament and it is through David that the
Messiah does come. He is made king over all
Israel.

In this section we must note that the Bible
records David's great sin and his repentance.
The Bible presents the total picture and paints
man as he is, not what he appears to be. We
do not find the sins of great men concealed or
excused in the Bible. It was the prophet of
God, Nathan, who had the courage to speak to
David about his sin. It is David's sin that
leads to all his thoughts recorded in the second
half of the book.

2. David's Troubles (Chapters 17-24)

Violence and incest within his own family were
the beginning of David's punishment for his
own twin sin of adultery and murder. Absalom,
David's son, leads a rebellion against his
father and tries to take over the kingdom. The
battle between David's troops and those of
Absalom ended with the death of Absalom at
the hands of Joab. The results of his sins
reached a culmination in his sorrow over
Absalom. David had further troubles within
the nation, but was finally re-established on
the throne.

B. MAIN CHARACTERS

1. David

2. Absalom

3. Joab

JOGGING NOTES

JOGGING RECORD SHEET
(Second Samuel)

SIN WILL TURN TRIUMPHS INTO TROUBLES

The Triumphs of David	The Troubles of David
Chapters 1 - 12	Chapters 13 - 24
King Over Judah at Hebron	Trouble in the Family
King Over All Israel at Jerusalem	Trouble in the Nation

BE SURE YOUR SINS WILL FIND YOU OUT

#		#	
1		13	
2		14	
3		15	
4		16	
5		17	
6		18	
7		19	
8		20	
9		21	
10		22	
11		23	
12		24	

JOGGING THROUGH FIRST KINGS

(The Decline and the Dividing of the Kingdom)

I. **FACTS TO KNOW**

    A. <u>TITLE</u>: The books (First and Second Kings record the events of the reign of the kings of Judah and Israel and thus the title - Kings.

    B. <u>WRITER</u>: Unknown. Tradition has Jeremiah writing both books with the aid of various sources.

    C. <u>KEY VERSES</u>: 2:12, 8:25

    D. <u>KEY WORD</u>: King (250 times)

    E. <u>DATE</u>: The two books cover a period of about 400 years, approximately 1000 - 600 B.C.

    F. <u>THEME</u>: The story of the growth, decay, decline, and collapse of the kingdom.

    G. <u>PURPOSE</u>: To record the history of Israel from the time of its greatest prosperity to its decline and fall.

II. **FOOD TO GROW**

    A. <u>FIRST KINGS TELLS ABOUT</u>:

        1. The Death of David (Chapters 1 - 2)

            The book opens with King David old and feeble. At seventy, he was prematurely aged and unable to reign with power. Taking advantage of the situation, David's oldest son, Adonijah, began a rebellion and coveted the throne. Such action called for a new king to be crowned before David's death. Moving quickly, Solomon, who was God's choice and more fit than Adonijah, was crowned king. Solomon was only 18 years old.

        2. The Reign of Solomon (Chapters 3 - 11)

            Solomon was a great and glorious king who asked God for wisdom and became the wisest man in the world. Under his wise leadership, the kingdom grew to the large dimensions out-

JOGGING NOTES

lined in Joshua -- nearly 60,000 square miles. The people were united, at peace with surrounding nations, and very prosperous. It was during this time of prosperity that Solomon forgot God and could only think of his possessions. Solomon had one of the greatest opportunities of any man to ever live, but he is one of the most colossal failures on the pages of scripture.

JOGGING NOTES

Solomon's failures were threefold:

  a. He forgot God when things were great
  b. He overburdened the people with taxes
  c. He had an undisciplined sexuality

3. The Building of the Temple (Chapters 5 - 8)

Solomon's greatest work was in the building of the temple at a cost of several million dollars. It took several years to build the temple and its dedication lasted seven days. It was patterned after the wilderness tabernacle and consisted of the Porch, the Holy Place, and the Holy of Holies.

4. The Division of the Kingdom (Chapters 12 - 22)

Rehoboam, son of Solomon, succeeds to the throne, and lays even heavier tax burdens on the people. Jeroboam returns from Egypt and leads 10 tribes in a tax revolt. There was continual war between Israel and Judah after the division.

5. The Ministry of Elijah

In the midst of the darkest period of Israel's turning against God, God's man appears on the scene. Elijah's mission is to bring the nation back to God and away from its sin. He confronts King Ahab, announces a three-year drought, raises the dead, and has a spectacular showdown with the prophets of Baal.

B. MAIN CHARACTERS

 1. Solomon

 2. Elijah

JOGGING RECORD SHEET
(First Kings)

THE DECLINE AND THE DIVIDING OF THE KINGDOM			
The Reign of Solomon, Chapters 1-11 Its Beginning Its Glory Its Failure		**Division of the Kingdom**, Chapters 12-22 The Disruption of the Nation The Ministry of Elijah	
1		12	
2		13	
3		14	
4		15	
5		16	
6		17	
7		18	
8		19	
9		20	
10		21	
11		22	

JOGGING THROUGH SECOND KINGS

(The Collapse of the Kingdoms and
the Captivity of God's People)

JOGGING NOTES

I. **FACTS TO KNOW**

   A. <u>RELATIONSHIP TO FIRST KINGS</u>: The second book of Kings continues the record begun in the first book of Kings. Ahaziah's reign in Israel began in First Kings and concludes in Second Kings. Second Kings continues the record of the divided kingdom from Ahab to the captivity. It describes the many kings, most of whom were wicked.

   B. <u>KEY VERSES</u>: 17:7-8; 18-23

II. **FOOD TO GROW**

   A. <u>SECOND KINGS TELLS ABOUT</u>:

   1. <u>The Ministry of Elisha</u>

      Elijah is taken up into heaven on a chariot of fire and Elisha is given his place. These great men of God stand in marked contrast to each other. Elijah is the fiery prophet of judgment and severity, while Elisha is the friendly prophet of grace and tenderness.

   2. <u>The Corruption of Israel</u>

      We are given a history of the kings of Israel and Judah, most of whom were bad and led the people away from God. Hezekiah and Josiah were good kings who sought to restore the true worship of God.

   3. <u>The Captivity</u>

      After some 250 years, the Northern Kingdom (Israel) was taken into captivity by Assyria. Some 136 years later, the Southern Kingdom was taken captive by Nebuchadnezzar, king of Babylon.

   Note: Israel was scattered among the nations for an indefinite period of time, but God specified that Judah's captivity would only last 70 years and that Judah would return to Jerusalem. God was using foreign rulers to work out His plan for the Messiah to come to Palestine and not Babylon or Assyria. The Messiah was to come out of Judah, the Davidic line.

JOGGING NOTES

B. <u>MAIN CHARACTERS</u>

   1. Elisha

   2. The Kings of Israel

   3. The Prophets of Israel

[Handwritten notes:]
586 B.C. Babalon destroyed Judah
Took people captive for 70 yrs. the Babalyon captivity.
722 B.C. Assyria attack & destroy Israel

JOGGING RECORD SHEET
(Second Kings)

THE COLLAPSE OF THE KINGDOMS AND THE CAPTIVITY OF GOD'S PEOPLE

  I. Events of Israel, the Northern Kingdom, Chapters 1 – 10
  II. Events of Both Kingdoms, Chapters 11 – 17
  III. Events of Judah, the Southern Kingdom, Chapters 18 – 25

#		#		#	
1		14			
2		15			
3		16			
4		17			
5		18			
6		19			
7		20			
8		21			
9		22			
10		23			
11		24			
12		25			
13					

JOGGING THROUGH FIRST CHRONICLES

JOGGING NOTES

A review from Adam to David - emphasizing the reign of David.

I. FACTS TO KNOW

   A. TITLE: The word means "record" or "journal."

   B. WRITER: According to Jewish tradition, Ezra is the writer.

   C. DATE: Probably between 450 and 400 B.C.

   D. RELATIONSHIP TO FORMER BOOKS: From Genesis through Second Kings, we have followed a chronological order of events -- from Adam's creation to Judah's captivity. Now, we come to a book that goes back and reviews the entire picture.

   E. RELATIONSHIP TO EZRA, NEHEMIAH, AND ESTHER: Originally I and II Chronicles, Ezra, and Nehemiah were one set of works. These books, along with Esther, form the four post-exile books (after the exile or captivity) and must be looked at as a group of books.

   F. PURPOSE AND THEME OF FIRST AND SECOND CHRONICLES: These books cover the same general period of history as Samuel and Kings, but from a spiritual viewpoint. It is a spiritual repetition of the history of the Davidic line with special reference to the temple, priests, and worship. Chronicles gives the history of Judah while practically ignoring the Northern Kingdom.

   G. KEY WORD: David (over 180 times)

   H. KEY VERSES: I Chronicles 29:26-27; 17:7-15

II. FOOD TO GROW

   A. FIRST CHRONICLES TELLS ABOUT:

      1. The Period from Adam to David (Chapters 1-20)

         The period from Adam to David is covered by genealogies. However, this list of genealogies is not a mere stringing together of names, but shows the purpose of God in the history of Israel.

2. The Reign of David (Chapters 11 - 21)

JOGGING NOTES

The review of the reign of David is given in narrative form and begins with Saul's last battle and death. Special attention is given to David's plans and preparation for the building of the temple. David gives Solomon the blueprint for building the temple and encourages him to build it. The last chapter records David's death and Solomon's ascension to the throne.

B. MAIN CHARACTER: David

JOGGING RECORD SHEET
(First Chronicles)

A REVIEW FROM ADAM TO DAVID			
I. The Review of History, Chapters 1 - 10 II. The Reign of David, Chapters 11 - 21			
1		12	
2		13	
3		14	
4		15	
5		16	
6		17	
7		18	
8		19	
9		20	
10		21	
11			

JOGGING THROUGH SECOND CHRONICLES

A review of the building of the temple - emphasizing the reign of Solomon.

I. **FACTS TO KNOW**

   A. See First Chronicles for information regarding both books. Second Chronicles is a continuation of First Chronicles with the same purpose and theme.

   B. <u>KEY VERSES</u>: II Chronicles 5:1; 36:14

   C. <u>KEY WORD</u>: Temple - "house of the Lord" (148 times)

II. **FOOD TO GROW**

   A. SECOND CHRONICLES TELLS ABOUT:

   1. <u>The Reign of Solomon</u> (Chapters 1 - 9)

      The first nine chapters review the reign of King Solomon and chapter 10 records the division of the kingdom.

   2. <u>The Building and Dedication of the Temple</u> (Chapters 2 - 9)

      First Chronicles records David's reign and his heartfelt desire to build the temple and Second Chronicles records Solomon's building of the temple, its services instituted, and the turning from God of the Jewish people.

   3. <u>The Kings of Judah Down to the Captivity</u> (Chapters 10 - 36)

      Following the dividing of the kingdom, the remainder of the book gives only the account of the Southern Kingdom of Judah. Special recognition is given to five good kings in whose regions were periods of <u>revival</u> and <u>renewal</u>.

   4. <u>The Decree of Cyrus</u> (Chapter 36)

      The book closes with the decree of Cyrus to allow Israel to return and to rebuild the temple at Jerusalem.

   B. MAIN CHARACTERS
      1. King Solomon
      2. Other Kings of Judah

JOGGING RECORD SHEET
(Second Chronicles)

A REVIEW OF THE BUILDING OF THE TEMPLE, EMPHASIZING THE REIGN OF SOLOMON

I. The Reign of Solomon, Chapters 1 – 9
II. The History of Judah to the Exile, Chapters 10 – 36

THE REVIVAL UNDER FIVE GOOD KINGS OF JUDAH

#		#	
1		19	
2		20	
3		21	
4		22	
5		23	
6		24	
7		25	
8		26	
9		27	
10		28	
11		29	
12		30	
13		31	
14		32	
15		33	
16		34	
17		35	
18		36	

JOGGABLE FIVE
LET'S JOG THROUGH THE RETURN AND RESTORATION

PERSIA CONQUERS BABYLON AND BECOMES DOMINANT POWER

1. King Cyrus issued a decree in 536 B.C. to allow the Jews to return to Jerusalem and to rebuild the temple.
2. Zerubbabel led the first group back to Jerusalem - a remnant of about 50,000.
3. Ezra, 60 years later, led the second group of about 1700 back to Jerusalem.
4. Nehemiah led the third group back and led them to rebuild the wall of Jerusalem.

MOST OF THE JEWS DID NOT RETURN TO JERUSALEM

1. They were settled and satisfied in Babylon.
2. Esther is the story of those who did not return (the majority).
3. Ezra-Nehemiah is the story of those who did return (the minority).

WORK ON THE TEMPLE STOPPED FOR 16 YEARS

1. Because of opposition, work stopped on the temple.
2. After 16 years, work on the temple was resumed under the encouragement of Haggai and Zechariah.

THREE PERSIAN KINGS WHO WERE FRIENDLY TO ISRAEL

1. Cyrus   2. Darius   3. Artaxerxes

THE TRIP BACK HOME

1. Some 800 miles of mostly desert.
2. Took four months to make the journey.

LENGTH OF CAPTIVITY

1. From the first departation to the return was exactly 70 years as predicted by the prophets and planned by God Himself.
2. It was God's plan to get His people back to Jerusalem because it was to Jerusalem and not Babylon that the Messiah would come.

LESSONS FROM CAPTIVITY

1. Cured of idolatry forever.
2. Had a new devotion for the temple.
3. Had a new appreciation for the scriptures

JOGGABLE FIVE

JOGGING THROUGH EZRA

JOGGING NOTES

(The Return and Restoration)

The people of Judah returning from captivity and rebuilding the temple at Jerusalem.

I. **FACTS TO KNOW**:

    A. WRITER: Tradition has ascribed Ezra as the writer of the book that bears his name. Ezra, a priest and scribe, came from exile in Babylon as leader of the second group that returned. *Rebuilding*

    B. RELATIONSHIP TO FORMER BOOKS: The books Ezra and Nehemiah were one book in the Hebrew Bible and continue the history of the book of Chronicles.

    C. KEY VERSES: Ezra 2:1; 6:21-22 *Priest & Scribe*

    D. KEY WORD: Jerusalem (47 times)

    E. PURPOSE: To give a historical record of the Jewish restoration of Jerusalem after the Babylonian captivity.

    F. THEME: The returning of the Jewish exiles to Jerusalem and the rebuilding of the temple.

II. **FOOD TO GROW**:

    A. EZRA TELLS ABOUT: *Governor*

        1. The Return Under Zerubbabel: (Chapters 1-6)

        The first six chapters tell the story of the historic return to Jerusalem by the Jews from their captivity in Babylon, under the leadership of Zerubbabel, the first governor appointed by Cyrus, King of Persia. However, most of the people are now settled and satisfied in Babylon, so only a remnant of about fifty thousand return.

        The alter of God was rebuilt; the offerings, sacrifices, and feasts days were restored, and work began on rebuilding the temple. Because of opposition, work on the temple was stopped for 16 years and resumed under the encour-

JOGGING NOTES

agement of Haggai and Zechariah. The temple was completed in the sixth year of Darius, King of Persia.

2. The Return Under Ezra (Chapters 7 - 10)

Ezra, some 60 years after the first group had returned, received a commission from Artaxerxes, the king, to lead all who wanted to return to Jerusalem. Finding the people in worse shape than he imagined, Ezra led the people in reforms.

B. EZRA IS A STORY OF FULFILLMENT

God raised up a new king, Cyrus, King of Persia, to be His instrument to get His people back in Jerusalem. Both Jeremiah and Isaiah had prophesied the capture and exile of Judah by Babylon, and the subsequent destruction of that cruel and wicked nation. Ezra shows how God presides over the destinies of men and nations.

JOGGING RECORD SHEET
(Ezra)

I. The Return Under Zerubbabel, Chapters 1 - 6
II. The Return Under Ezra, Chapters 7 - 10

1		6	
2		7	
3		8	
4		9	
5		10	

JOGGING THROUGH NEHEMIAH

(Return and Restoration)

Nehemiah continues where Ezra left off with the story of the restoration and is the last of the historical books, bringing us to the close of the Old Testament.

I. FACTS TO KNOW

   A. WRITER: Nehemiah

   B. THEME: The story of a great man of God and his courageous commitment to rebuild the walls of Jerusalem and continue the reforms of Ezra in the face of tremendous opposition.

   C. PURPOSE: To give a historical account of the rebuilding of the walls of Jerusalem and the completion of Ezra's reformation.

   D. KEY VERSES: Nehemiah 1:4; 4:6; 6:3

II. FOOD TO GROW

   A. NEHEMIAH TELLS ABOUT:

   1. Rebuilding the Walls (Chapters 1 - 7)

      Nehemiah, cupbearer to Artaxerxes, King of Persia, was appointed by the king as the new governor of Judah. He led the third group of exiles from captivity and his main purpose was to rebuild the wall of Jerusalem and restore Jerusalem as a fortified city. In spite of constant opposition, Nehemiah led the people to rebuild the wall in record time (52 days). He did this by combining continuous work with cautious defense.

   2. Renewing the Covenant. (Chapters 8 - 13)

      Ezra stands upon a pulpit of wood and reads the law from morning until noon. The people make and sign a covenant to serve God and walk in all His ways.

   B. THE MAIN CHARACTER: NEHEMIAH

   Nehemiah was God's man of the hour -- a man of courage, concern, caution, and commitment. He would make no compromise with the enemies within the temple or within the city, or with those without. He stood solidly on God's Word and had faith to act with God and for God. He feared only God.

JOGGING NOTES

JOGGING RECORD SHEET
(Nehemiah)

I. Rebuilding the Walls, Chapters 1 – 7		
II. Renewing the Covenant, Chapters 8 – 13		
1	8	
2	9	
3	10	
4	11	
5	12	
6	13	
7		

JOGGING THROUGH ESTHER — Remaining

(Return and Restoration)

JOGGING NOTES

A short story showing the deliverance of Israel from destruction by the overruling power of God.

I. **FACTS TO KNOW**

   A. TITLE: Taken from its principle character, Esther, a Jewish maiden who became queen of a Persian king, and through whose efforts the Jews were preserved from destruction.

   B. WRITER: Unknown. Mordecai has been suggested. (9:20)

   C. SETTING: The palace and court of the King of Persia

   D. KEY VERSE: Esther 4:14

   E. PURPOSE: To record the divine deliverance of dispersed Jews during the reign of Persian King Ahasuerus (485-465 B.C.) and to show God's providential care of His children.

   F. DATE: Chronologically, the book comes after Nehemiah, but the events precede Nehemiah by about 30 years.

   G. THEME: The providence of God

II. **FOOD TO GROW**

   A. ESTHER TELLS ABOUT:

   1. The Great Danger (Chapters 1 - 5)

      These first chapters reveal a carefully laid out plot to destroy all the Jews throughout Persia.

   2. The Great Deliverance (Chapters 6 - 10)

      The carefully laid plot was miraculously frustrated and instead of the Jews, it was their enemies who were destroyed. Instead of Mordecai, it was the wicked Haman who died on the gallows.

   B. ESTHER AND NEHEMIAH

      Esther's marriage to the king gave prestige to the Jews and in one way made possible the work of Nehemiah. Without Esther, Jerusalem might never have been rebuilt and the Jewish race would have been slain.

      Esther is the story of those who did not return (majority) and Ezra-Nehemiah is the story of those who did return (remnant-minority).

JOGGING RECORD SHEET
(Esther)

I. The Great Danger, Chapters 1 – 5
II. The Great Deliverance, Chapters 6 – 10

1		6	
2		7	
3		8	
4		9	
5		10	

JOGGABLE SIX
LET'S JOG THROUGH THE POETS AND PROPHETS

Isaiah "Prince of Prophets"

THE NATURE OF HEBREW POETRY

1. It is free verse
2. It is musical (rhythmic).
3. It is highly figurative.

A COMPARISON

HISTORICAL SECTION	POETICAL SECTION
17 books	5 books
history	experience
nation	individuals
Hebrew race	human heart
manner	mood

THE BOOKS OF POETRY

Job
Psalms
Proverbs
Ecclesiastes
Song of Solomon

417 – 2400 yrs

800 BC
400 BC

MESSAGE
1. Chosen
2. Captured
3. Captivity — Daniel
4. Coming

NUMBER
1. Major (5)
2. Minor (12)

MINISTRY
1. Forthtelling
2. Foretelling

TIME SPAN
1. 800–400 B.C. (Est.)
2. Bad kings
3. Disobedient people
4. Corrupt priests

JOGGABLE SIX

JOGGING THROUGH JOB

(Poetry)

THE POETICAL BOOKS

HISTORY	POETRY	PROPHETS
MANNER	MOOD	MESSAGE

JOGGING NOTES
Ecclesiastic
Living on the Ragged Edge.

There are five books in the Old Testament usually classified as poetry: Job, Psalms, Ecclesiastes, and Song of Solomon. The term "poetry" only refers to their form and in no way implies that they are the products of human imagination. These books deal with real human experience and grapple with difficult problems. Until now, we have been dealing with a nation and now, we are dealing with individuals.

I. **FACTS TO KNOW**

   A. <u>WRITER</u>: Unknown. Suggestions include Elihu, Moses, and Job.

   B. <u>DATE</u>: Uncertain

   C. <u>KEY VERSES</u>: Job 1:21; 13:15; 14:14; 19:25; 42:6

   D. <u>PURPOSE</u>: To show divine and human reasoning regarding the problem of human suffering.

   E. <u>THEME</u>: Man, through suffering, is tested and triumphant.

II. **FOOD TO GROW**

   A. JOB TELLS ABOUT:

   1. <u>Satan</u>

      Satan is introduced as a powerful, but limited being, who is given permission to test Job by inflicting him with adversity. He hurls every evil he knows at the man about whom the Lord said "There is none like him in the earth."

   2. <u>Suffering</u>

      Job loses his children and property in a single day. He next loses his health and then his

65

LOGGING NOTES

good name. Yet, in spite of his great suffering, he never sinned with his lips. His reply: "The Lord giveth and the Lord taketh away. Blessed be the name of the Lord."

3. The Advice of Friends

Job's three friends, Eliphaz, Bildad, and Zophar arrive to comfort him and we have recorded three cycles of speeches. In essence, they all believe that God sends suffering as a punishment for sin.

4. Job's Repentance

For 41 chapters, Job had maintained that he had done no wrong. It is not until chapter 42 that we find Job in the presence of God confessing his sin and repenting. As a result, God gives Job twice as much as he had at the beginning.

B. LESSONS FROM JOB

1. The real cause and purpose of suffering is not always clear.

2. Suffering is a test of righteousness and faith.

3. Suffering leads a believer to a deeper understanding of God, of himself, and of his needs.

4. Satan is the author of suffering, but God permits it and can overrule it for His own purpose.

JOGGING RECORD SHEET
(Job)

I. The Prologue, Chapters 1 – 2
II. The Dialogue, Chapters 3 – 42:6
III. The Epilogue, Chapters 42: 7 – 17

#		#		#	
1		22			
2		23			
3		24			
4		25			
5		26			
6		27			
7		28			
8		29			
9		30			
10		31			
11		32			
12		33			
13		34			
14		35			
15		36			
16		37			
17		38			
18		39			
19		40			
20		41			
21		42			

JOGGING THROUGH PSALMS

"The Hymnbook of the Nation, Israel."

I. **FACTS TO KNOW**

    A. **TITLE**: The Hebrew title of the book is "Book of Praises," so called because it is a devotional manual for public and private worship. "Psalms" comes from the Greek and suggests an instrumental accompaniment. A songbook for Christians.

    B. **AUTHOR**: The universal tradition is that David wrote most of the Psalms. He is named as the author of 73, while 50 more are anonymous. Among the various authors of the remaining Psalms, we find Solomon and Moses.

    C. **PURPOSE**: To provide a book of devotion for the people of God. Written to be sung, it became the hymnbook for the nation of Israel.

    D. **THEME**: Worship through prayer.

    E. **DATE**: From before the time of David until the restoration of Israel under Ezra and Nehemiah, certain men talked with God about their deepest hurts and greatest joys. (About 1030 - 403 B.C.)

    F. **ARRANGEMENT**: The Psalms are arranged in five books.
        1. Book I   - Psalms 1 - 41
        2. Book II - Psalms 42 - 72
        3. Book III - Psalms 73 - 89
        4. Book IV - Psalms 90 - 106
        5. Book V - Psalms 107 - 150

II. **FOOD TO GROW**

    A. **THE PSALMS TELL ABOUT**:

        1. **The Gospel**

        In each of the five divisions, one will find cries for rescue from sin and misery, songs commemorating divine deliverance, and songs of praise and gratitude.

JOGGING NOTES

JOGGING NOTES

2. Life

The Psalms touch all of life and deal with the cause and cure of every problem known to man. The Psalms move from the depths to the heights in expressing the varying emotions of the human heart.

B. THE MESSIANIC PSALMS

Many of the Psalms refer, by prophetic anticipation, to Jesus Christ and therefore, must be interpreted in light of the New Testament.

JOGGING RECORD SHEET
(Psalms)

WORSHIPING GOD THROUGH PRAYER AND PRAISE

Psalms of Praise	Psalms of Prophecy
Psalms of Thanksgiving	Psalms of Trust
Psalms of Wisdom	Psalms of God's Greatness
Psalms of Repentance	Psalms of Patriotism
Psalms of Captivity	Psalms of the Wicked
Psalms of Freedom	Psalms of Trouble
Psalms of Law	Psalms of Pilgrimages

1		22		43		64		85	
2		23		44		65		86	
3		24		45		66		87	
4		25		46		67		88	
5		26		47		68		89	
6		27		48		69		90	
7		28		49		70		91	
8		29		50		71		92	
9		30		51		72		93	
10		31		52		73		94	
11		32		53		74		95	
12		33		54		75		96	
13		34		55		76		97	
14		35		56		77		98	
15		36		57		78		99	
16		37		58		79		100	
17		38		59		80		101	
18		39		60		81		102	
19		40		61		82		103	
20		41		62		83		104	
21		42		63		84		105	
								106	

107		129	
108		130	
109		131	
110		132	
111		133	
112		134	
113		135	
114		136	
115		137	
116		138	
117		139	
118		140	
119		141	
120		142	
121		143	
122		144	
123		145	
124		146	
125		147	
126		148	
127		149	
128		150	

JOGGING THROUGH PROVERBS
(Heavenly Advice for Earthly Living)

I. FACTS TO KNOW

    A. WRITER: Most of the Proverbs are from Solomon

    B. DATE: Between 950 B.C. and 725 B.C.

    C. PURPOSE: To apply divine wisdom to daily life in an evil world.

    D. THEME: Spiritual wisdom

II. FOOD TO GROW

    A. PROVERBS TELLS ABOUT:

        1. People Who Really Need Wisdom

            a. The Fool

            b. The Simple

            c. The Scorner

        2. People Who Really Are Wise

        3. The Path of True Wisdom

    B. PROVERBS GIVES A CONTRAST BETWEEN FOLLY AND WISDOM

        1. Wisdom Is Rooted in the Fear of the Lord and Produces Virtue

        2. Folly Is Rooted in Self-Will and Produces Vice

JOGGING NOTES

JOGGING RECORD SHEET
(Proverbs)

I.	The Wisdom of Solomon (Especially for the Young)
II.	The Wisdom of Solomon (For All Men)
III.	The Wisdom of Solomon (Copied by Hezekiah's Men)
IV.	The Wisdom of Others (Appendix)

#		#	
1		17	
2		18	
3		19	
4		20	
5		21	
6		22	
7		23	
8		24	
9		25	
10		26	
11		27	
12		28	
13		29	
14		30	
15		31	
16			

JOGGING THROUGH ECCLESIASTES — *Preaching*

JOGGING NOTES

I. **FACTS TO KNOW**

   A. <u>WRITER</u>: Solomon, the most powerful king to reign over Israel.

   B. <u>PURPOSE</u>: To teach the emptiness of everything apart from God.

   C. <u>KEY VERSES</u>: Ecclesiastes 2:11; 12:12-14

   D. <u>KEY WORD</u>: Vanity

II. **FOOD TO GROW**

   A. <u>ECCLESIASTES TELLS ABOUT</u>:

      1. The Vanity of Human Wisdom

      2. The Vanity of Pleasure

      3. The Vanity of Materialism

Human effort

   B. <u>ECCLESIASTES REPRESENTS THE PHILOSOPHY OF THE WORLD ITSELF</u>

      1. A "Do the Best You Can" Philosophy Based on Worldly Wisdom and Self-Interest

      2. The World Cannot Satisfy the Heart, Only the Son of God Can.

JOGGING RECORD SHEET
(Ecclesiastes)

I. <u>Introduction and Theme</u>, Chapter 1:1-11
II. <u>Experimentation</u>, Chapters 1:12 - 2:26
III. <u>Observation</u>, Chapters 3:1 - 8:15
IV. <u>Application and Conclusion</u>, Chapters 8:16 - 12:14

#		#		
1		7		
2		8		
3		9		
4		10		
5		11		
6		12		

JOGGING THROUGH SONG OF SOLOMON — *Delighting in wedded love.*

JOGGING NOTES

I. FACTS TO KNOW

- A. **WRITER**: Solomon, King of Israel
- B. **KEY VERSE**: Solomon 6:3
- C. **KEY WORD**: Love
- D. **DATE**: About 1000 B.C.
- E. **PURPOSE**: To show the love of Jehovah for Israel, and of Christ for the Church.
- F. **KEY TO UNDERSTANDING**: It is a poem of wedded love in oriental language and imagery and must be interpreted in that light.

II. FOOD TO GROW

The true value and appreciation of this love song is reserved for those whose hearts are devoted to Christ. It must be understood that in oriental poetry the physical charms of lovers are minutely described without any thought of vulgarity. Spiritually, this song of wedded love portrays the communion between Christ and the individual believer.

JOGGING RECORD SHEET
(The Song of Solomon)

	"I AM LOVED"
1	Int. in 4 ways. — Literally (wedded love)
2	Israel (God's love)
3	Christ (Christ's) love for church
4	Individual & Christ's love.
5	
6	
7	
8	

JOGGING THROUGH ISAIAH

Prophet of Salvation in old testament.

JOGGING NOTES

Isaiah lived 800 B.C.

I. **FACTS TO KNOW**

   A. <u>WRITER</u>:   Isaiah, an eighth century prophet of Judah.

   B. <u>DATE</u>: Uncertain

   C. <u>(KEY WORD</u>): Salvation - *Saving*

   D. <u>KEY VERSE</u>: Isaiah 7:14

   E. <u>PURPOSE</u>:   To speak against the idolatry and social sins of that day and to predict the captivity, restoration, and the glories of a coming Messianic age.

   F. <u>THEME</u>: Salvation through judgment and grace.

II. **FOOD TO GROW**

   A. ISAIAH TELLS ABOUT:

   1. The (Captivity)

      Isaiah, by a miracle of inspiration, speaks as a contemporary of the Babylonian exile and predicts pardon, deliverance, and restoration.

   2. The Cross

      The 53rd chapter of Isaiah gives us one of the clearest views of Calvary in all of God's Word. The cross is at the very heart of Isaiah's message.

   B. MAIN CHARACTER: Isaiah

   The secret of Isaiah's power and effective ministry can be seen in his vision in the temple (chapter six).

JOGGING RECORD SHEET
(Isaiah)

I.	Judgment and Denunciation Chapters 1-39		
II.	Grace and Consolation Chapters 40-66		

#		#	
1		26	
2		27	
3		28	
4		29	
5		30	
6		31	
7		32	
8		33	
9		34	
10		35	
11		36	
12		37	
13		38	
14		39	
15		40	
16		41	
17		42	
18		43	
19		44	
20		45	
21		46	
22		47	
23		48	
24		49	
25		50	

ISAIAH

51		59	
52		60	
53		61	
54		62	
55		63	
56		64	
57		65	
58		66	

JOGGING THROUGH JEREMIAH

JOGGING NOTES

I. **FACTS TO KNOW**

   A. <u>WRITER</u>: Jeremiah, a prophet to Judah for some 40 years.

   B. <u>PURPOSE</u>: To warn of impending judgment and captivity.

   C. <u>KEY WORDS</u>: Sin, captivity, and Babylon.

   D. <u>DATE</u>: Uncertain. His ministry was from about 626 - 586 B.C.

   E. <u>KEY VERSES</u>: Jeremiah 1:18-19; 21:7, 14

II. **FOOD TO GROW**

   A. JEREMIAH TELLS ABOUT:

   1. The Spiritual and Moral Conditions

      It was a dark day of moral rottenness and spiritual decay caused primarily by bad kings, apathetic people, corrupt priests, and false prophets.

   2. The Captivity and Restoration

      Although the people were already doomed to captivity, Jeremiah gave some glorious Messianic prophecies predicting that the captivity would end after 70 years with repentance and restoration.

   B. MAIN CHARACTER: Jeremiah

JOGGING RECORD SHEET
(Jeremiah)

   I. The Call and Commission, Chapter 1
  II. Prophecies Before the Fall of Jerusalem, Chapters 2 - 38
 III. The Fall of Jerusalem, Chapter 39
  IV. Prophecies After the Fall of Jerusalem, Chapters 40 - 45
   V. Prophecies Concerning the Nations, Chapters 46 - 51
  VI. Historical Appendix, Chapter 52

#		#		#	
1		27			
2		28			
3		29			
4		30			
5		31			
6		32			
7		33			
8		34			
9		35			
10		36			
11		37			
12		38			
13		39			
14		40			
15		41			
16		42			
17		43			
18		44			
19		45			
20		46			
21		47			
22		48			
23		49			
24		50			
25		51			
26		52			

JOGGING THROUGH LAMENTATIONS

JOGGING NOTES

I. **FACTS TO KNOW**

    A. <u>WRITER</u>: Jeremiah. A supplement to the book of Jeremiah.

    B. <u>DATE</u>: About 589 – 587 B.C., before the destruction of Jerusalem.

    C. <u>THEME</u>: The lamenting over Judah's sins and her subsequent captivity.

    D. <u>PURPOSE</u>: To commemorate the death of Jerusalem and to reveal the suffering heart of God over sin.

    E. <u>KEY VERSE</u>: Lamentations 1:1

II. <u>**FOOD TO GROW**</u>

The book is a collection of five poems in the form of a funeral address commemorating the fall of Jerusalem to the Babylonians in 586 B.C. The grief of Jeremiah is also God's grief.

JOGGING RECORD SHEET
(Lamentations)

I.	The Affliction and Sorrow of Captivity, Chapter 1
II.	The Anger of God Against Sin, Chapter 2
III.	The Cry of Jeremiah for Mercy, Chapter 3
IV.	The Judgment of God Against Sin, Chapter 4
V.	The Prayer of Jerusalem for Mercy, Chapter 5

1	
2	
3	
4	
5	

JOGGING THROUGH EZEKIEL — *unfailing*

JOGGING NOTES

I. **FACTS TO KNOW**

    A. <u>WRITER</u>: Ezekiel, a prophet of the captivity.

    B. <u>DATE</u>: Uncertain

    C. <u>KEY VERSES</u>: Ezekiel 36:17-19, 24-28

    D. <u>PURPOSE</u>: To show the people of God three important things:

        1. The awfulness of their sins
        2. The severity of God's judgment
        3. The unfailing promise of God's blessing

    E. <u>THEME</u>: The revelation of Jehovah as the one true God.

II. **FOOD TO GROW**

    A. <u>EZEKIEL TELLS ABOUT</u>:

        1. The punishment of Jerusalem and the captivity of God's people.

        2. The judgment against the Gentile nations of Ezekiel's day.

        3. The preservation and ultimate restoration of the covenant people.

    B. <u>EZEKIEL IS THE PROPHET OF THE "GLORY OF THE LORD."</u>

        1. He saw the "Shekinah" glory of the Lord leave Solomon's temple and he saw the return of the glory of the Lord in the coming future kingdom.

        2. He dramatized (acted out) the message of God in order to get the attention of a rebellious nation in its darkest days.

        3. Ezekiel's prophetic utterances were in the form of visions, signs, and direct prophecies.

        4. He is one of the three prophets (Daniel, John, and Ezekiel) who spoke from without the land. All three used highly symbolic language to describe the most profound visions ever given to mortal men.

JOGGING RECORD SHEET
(Ezekiel)

I. Prophecies Before the Fall of Jerusalem, Chapters 1 - 24
II. Judgment Upon Foreign Nations, Chapters 25 - 32
III. Prophecies After the Fall of Jerusalem, Chapters 33 - 48

#		#		#	
1		25			
2		26			
3		27			
4		28			
5		29			
6		30			
7		31			
8		32			
9		33			
10		34			
11		35			
12		36			
13		37			
14		38			
15		39			
16		40			
17		41			
18		42			
19		43			
20		44			
21		45			
22		46			
23		47			
24		48			

Last half of Daniel is apocalyptic

JOGGING THROUGH DANIEL — *Interpreting*

JOGGING NOTES

Daniel had purpose, prayer, prophecy

Daniel & Rev. go hand in hand.

Babylon called city of Gold

I. **FACTS TO KNOW**

  A. WRITER: Daniel, the prophet-statesman of Jehovah God, during the captivity.

  B. DATE OF MINISTRY: 606 - 534 B.C.

  D. PURPOSE: To show that Jehovah God controls and directs the affairs of man, the forces of nature, and the history of nations for the accomplishment of His divine plan.

  D. THEME: The sovereignty of God.

  E. KEY WORD: King

  F. KEY VERSES: Daniel 1:8; 2:21; 2:47

II. **FOOD TO GROW**

  A. DANIEL TELLS ABOUT:

   1. **The Future**
      The second chapter of Daniel gives us the most complete picture in all the Bible of what will come to pass in the future. In the form of a great image, God reveals the Gentile powers, four great empires, that were to succeed each other in the government of the world from Babylon to the end. The last government will be the weakest and will end in utter chaos. Then Christ will come and set up a kingdom that will last forever and ever.

   2. **Himself**
      We know more about Daniel than any of the other prophets due to the fact that he gives us a personal history from 606 B.C. to 534 B.C. Daniel is the "Mr. Clean" of the Old Testament, a man of purpose, prayer, and prophecy, who remains totally consistant to God in a vile and pagan court. This remarkable young man rose in power to become prime minister of Babylon.

   3. **Babylon**
      Babylon, the wonder city of the ancient world, came to its power during the time of Daniel, by Nebuchadnezzar -- Daniel's friend who reigned for 45 years.

  B. MAIN CHARACTER: Daniel

85

JOGGING RECORD SHEET
(Daniel)

FAITHFULNESS TO GOD WHATEVER THE COST	
PERSONAL HISTORY (3rd Person) Chapters 1 – 6	**PROPHETIC MINISTRY** (1st Person) Chapters 7 – 12
THE PROMISE OF ULTIMATE VICTORY	

1		7	
2		8	
3		9	
4		10	
5		11	
6		12	

JOGGING THROUGH HOSEA — Wooing

JOGGING NOTES

I. FACTS TO KNOW

   A. WRITER: Hosea, an eighth century prophet of divine love, who is called "the Jeremiah of the Northern Kingdom." He is the only writing prophet of the Northern Kingdom to address his own people.

   1-3 unfaithful wife

   B. PURPOSE: To show the faithfulness of God's love toward an unfaithful Israel and to warn of a coming judgment and a future restoration.

   4-11 unfaithful nation

   C. THEME: Israel's unfaithfulness to God is illustrated in terms of a wife (Gomer), who has turned her back upon a faithful husband, (Hosea), in order to follow evil lovers.

   12-14 faithful God.

   D. DATE OF WRITING: Between 786 and 725 B.C. and before the Assyrian captivity in 722 B.C.

   E. KEY WORDS: Whoredom, lovingkindness, and return

II. FOOD TO GROW

   A. HOSEA TELLS ABOUT:

      1. The Unfaithfulness of God's People

         Israel had reached its lowest level of immorality and idolatry and had become insensitive to sin. Into this darkness, God had sent Elijah, Elisha, Jonah, Amos, and now, Hosea. Sin not only breaks God's law but it breaks His heart.

      2. A Future Restoration

         Israel, the now disowned wife of God, will one day be repentant, forgiven, and restored. This is a book for backsliders, a lesson on repentance.

   B. KEY TO UNDERSTANDING HOSEA

      The book of Hosea is more poetical than many of the prophets and abounds in striking metaphors. Israel is Jehovah's bride, as the church is the bride of Christ. Therefore, she should bind herself faithfully to Him alone – to worship and obey.

JOGGING RECORD SHEET
(Hosea)

SIN	PUNISHMENT	RESTORATION
	I. The Unfaithful Wife, Chapters 1 - 3 II. The Unfaithful Nation, Chapters 4 - 11 III. The Faithful God, Chapters 12 - 14	
	A LOVE THAT WILL NEVER LET GO	
1	8	
2	9	
3	10	
4	11	
5	12	
6	13	
7	14	

JOGGING THROUGH JOEL — Repenting

JOGGING NOTES
chp.
2¹-11
punishment
18 on
promise

I. **FACTS TO KNOW**

   A. **WRITER**: Joel, a little known prophet of God.

   B. **DATE**: Uncertain

   C. **KEY VERSES**: Joel 2:28-32

   D. **PURPOSE**: To show cause (Israel's sin) for the terrible plague and to call the nation back to God.

   E. **THEME**: "The Coming of the Lord."

II. **FOOD TO GROW**

   A. **JOEL TELLS ABOUT**:

   1. The Terrible Plague

      As a judgment of God, locusts swarmed the earth and devoured every green thing in their path. The plague, a literal event and symbolic of the future wrath of God, brought the people to their knees in repentance. God answered their prayer and removed the locusts.

   2. The Future

      God will one day judge all nations for any wrongs they have done Israel and Israel will be restored and renewed.

   B. **A SCARLET THREAD OF GRACE**

   Even though the basic message of the book is judgment, there is a thread of grace running through the book. There is coming a day of grace, which precedes the final judgment of God, and is to be ushered in by the outpouring of the Holy Spirit (See Acts 2:14).

JOGGING RECORD SHEET
(Joel)

THE OUTPOURING OF THE HOLY SPIRIT
I. The Punishment (Plague of Locusts), Chapters 1:1 - 2:11
II. The Penitence, Chapter 2:12 - 17
III. The Promises, Chapters 2:18 - 3:21

	THE COMING DAY
1	
2	
3	

JOGGING THROUGH AMOS

I. **FACTS TO KNOW**

    A. **WRITER**: Amos, a layman (farmer) called to deliver God's message.

    B. **DATE**: Between 785 and 750 B.C., some 30 years before the fall of Israel.

    C. **PURPOSE**: To predict punishment for foreign nations and to warn Israel of impending judgment for its immorality and idolatry.

    D. **THEME**: The certain judgment of God upon sin.

    E. **KEY VERSES**: Amos 3:2; 4:11-12

    F. **KEY WORDS**: Punishment, captivity, transgression

II. **FOOD TO GROW**

    A. **AMOS TELLS ABOUT**:

        1. The Judgment Against the Foreign Nations

        2. The Judgment Against Israel

        3. The Future of Israel

    B. **AMOS DESCRIBES**

        1. The Sin in the Sanctuary

        2. The Insult of Worship Without Obedience

    C. **AMOS PREDICTS**

        1. The Fall of Israel and the Captivity of God's People

        2. The Future Restoration of God's People and the Glory of the Messianic Kingdom

JOGGING NOTES

JOGGING RECORD SHEET
(Amos)

GOD WILL PUNISH SIN
I. Judgment Against the Nations in General, Chapters 1 – 2 II. Judgment Against Israel, in Particular, Chapters 5 – 6 III. Visions Concerning Israel, Chapters 7 – 9 IV. Promised Concerning Israel, Chapter 9:11 – 15

1	
2	
3	
4	
5	
6	
7	
8	
9	

JOGGING THROUGH OBADIAH

JOGGING NOTES

I. **FACTS TO KNOW**

   A. **WRITER**: Obadiah, a little known prophet of God.

   B. **DATE**: Uncertain. Possibly just after the destruction of Jerusalem.

   C. **PURPOSE**: To prophesy against Edom (small nation and descendants of Essau) for refusing Israel passage through their country (Numbers 2:14-21) and for looking on while Jerusalem was being destroyed and evidently enjoying it.

   D. **THEME**: The coming day of Edom's destruction and Judah's ultimate salvation.

II. **FOOD TO GROW**

   A. **OBADIAH TELLS ABOUT**:

     1. Edom and the Edomites

     2. God's Love, Patience, and Providential Care of His People

     3. The Necessity of Punishing Sinful Pride and Godless Rebellion

   B. **SPIRITUAL TYPES**

     1. Essau, <u>rebellious</u> man, represents man's fleshly nature

     2. Jacob, <u>religious</u> man, represents the people of God

     3. Edom, <u>ruined</u> man, represents the world and its enmity toward God

JOGGING RECORD SHEET
(Obadiah)

THE ROCKS FAIL (FALSE SECURITY)

I. Edom's Doom Announced, Chapters 1 - 9
II. Edom's Guilt Declared, Chapters 10 - 16
III. Judah's Future Foretold, Chapters 17 - 21

THE KINGDOM ENDURES (TRUE FOUNDATION)

JOGGING THROUGH JONAH

JOGGING NOTES

I. **FACTS TO KNOW**

    A. <u>WRITER</u>: Jonah, one of the earliest writing prophets.

    B. <u>DATE OF WRITING</u>: 785 - 767 B.C., during reign of Jeroboam II.

    C. <u>PURPOSE</u>: To teach God's people that He was God of the Gentiles and that He would respond in grace and love to any genuinely repentant nation.

    D. <u>THEME</u>: The personal history of a man called of God to preach to the Gentiles.

    E. <u>KEY VERSES</u>: Jonah 1:12; 3:2, 3 - 5

II. **FOOD TO GROW**

    A. <u>JONAH TELLS ABOUT</u>:

       1. Jonah's Call and Disobedience (Chapter 1)

       2. Jonah's Punishment, Repentance, and Deliverance (Chapter 2)

       3. Jonah's Call and Obedience (Chapter 3)

       4. Jonah's Resentment and God's Rebuke (Chapter 4)

    B. **SPIRITUAL TYPES**

       1. Jonah Is a Type of Christ in His Death, Burial, and Resurrection

       2. Jonah Is a Type of Israel, Disobedient to God and Cast Into the Sea of Nations and Swallowed By the Nations of the World.

    C. **KEY TO UNDERSTANDING**

    Jonah did not disobey God out of cowardice, but out of a false patriotism. Assyria (Ninevah was the capital) was Israel's great enemy.

JOGGING RECORD SHEET
(Jonah)

TRUST AND OBEY
I. Jonah's Call and Disobedience, Chapter 1 II. Jonah's Punishment, Prayer, and Deliverance, Chapter 2 III. Jonah's Call and Obedience, Chapter 3 IV. Jonah's Resentment and God's Rebuke, Chapter 4
GOD'S LOVE AND MERCY IS FOR ALL

1	
2	
3	
4	

JOGGING THROUGH MICAH

JOGGING NOTES

I. **FACTS TO KNOW**

   A. **WRITER**: Micah

   B. **DATE**: Uncertain

   C. **KEY VERSES**: Micah 4:3, 6:8

   D. **KEY WORD**: Remnant

   E. **PURPOSE**: To warn against sin in both kingdoms, to predict a coming judgment, and to proclaim a future restoration.

   F. **THEME**: The judgment and redemption of God

II. **FOOD TO GROW**

   A. **MICAH TELLS ABOUT**:

   1. The Coming Judgment
   2. The Coming Kingdom

   B. **MICAH DEFINES**:

   1. True Religion (6:8)
   2. The Requirements of God (6:1 - 7:7)

JOGGING RECORD SHEET
(Micah)

	I. The Coming Judgment, Chapters 1 - 3 II. The Coming Kingdom, Chapters 4 - 5 III. The Controversy and Final Appeal, Chapters 6 - 7
1	
2	
3	
4	

JOGGING THROUGH NAHUM

JOGGING NOTES

I. **FACTS TO KNOW**

   A. <u>WRITER</u>: Nahum, little known prophet of God

   B. <u>DATE</u>: Uncertain, probably written between 663 and 612 B.C.

   C. <u>PURPOSE</u>: To pronounce the judgment of God upon Ninevah and to comfort Judah with the promise of future deliverance.

   D. <u>THEME</u>: The destruction of Ninevah, the capital city of Assyria.

   E. <u>KEY VERSES</u>: Nahum 1:1; 1:7-8; 3:5-7

   F. <u>KEY WORDS</u>: Doom, vengeance, and Ninevah

II. **FOOD TO GROW**

   A. <u>NAHUM TELLS ABOUT</u>:

      1. The Judge (1:1-7)

      2. The Judgment (1:8 - 3:19)

   B. <u>KEY TO UNDERSTANDING</u>:

   The book of Nahum forms a beautiful poem describing the "other side" of God - His vengeance. While Jonah pictures God's love, forgiveness, and salvation, Nahum pictures God's holiness, judgment, and destruction.

JOGGING RECORD SHEET
(Nahum)

GOD IS LOVING AND FORGIVING
I. The Judge, Chapter 1:1 - 7 II. The Judgment, Chapters 1:8 - 3:19
GOD IS JEALOUS AND AVENGING

1	
2	
3	

JOGGING THROUGH HABAKKUK *complaining*

I. **FACTS TO KNOW**

    A. <u>WRITER</u>: Habakkuk, a little known prophet to Judah.

    B. <u>DATE</u>: Uncertain. Possibly around 607 B.C.

    C. <u>PURPOSE</u>: To deal with the problem of why the wicked prosper.

    D. <u>THEME</u>: "The just shall live by faith."

II. **FOOD TO GROW**

    A. <u>HABAKKUK TELLS ABOUT</u>:

        1. The Spiritual Condition of Judah.

            It was a day of dark apostasy (1:2-4). The last three rulers were evil and idolatry was everywhere.

        2. <u>God</u>

            Most of the book is a conversation between Habakkuk and God. It asserts God's righteousness and holiness as the standard for judging the world.

    B. THE MESSAGE OF FAITH

        1. The Words "The Just Shall Live By Faith" Are To Be Found Three Times in the New Testament.

        2. The Enemy Will Be Ultimately Punished and the "Just" Will Be Preserved in the Time of Trouble. God's Promise Is the Basis for our Faith.

JOGGING NOTES

2-3-4
Hab. complaint

5-11
God's answer

vs. 12
2nd complaint

5 woes to Babalayn

chp. 3
Habakuk prayer

JOGGING RECORD SHEET
(Habakkuk)

QUESTION: "WHAT IS GOD DOING?"
I. Habakkuk's Complaint and God's Answer, Chapter 1:1 – 11   II. Habakkuk's Second Complaint and God's Answer, Chapters 1:1 – 2:20   III. Habakkuk's Prayer, Chapter 3
ANSWER: THE JUST SHALL LIVE BY FAITH

1	
2	
3	

JOGGING THROUGH ZEPHANIAH

JOGGING NOTES

I. **FACTS TO KNOW**

    A. <u>WRITER</u>: Zephaniah, a little known prophet of Judah.

    B. <u>PURPOSE</u>: To warn Judah of the coming "day of the Lord."

    C. <u>THEME</u>: The coming day of God's wrath

    D. <u>DATE</u>: Uncertain. Zephaniah was the last of the prophets before captivity and was contemporary with Jeremiah.

II. **FOOD TO GORW**

    A. ZEPHANIAH TELLS ABOUT:

        1. <u>The Coming Day of God's Wrath</u>

        This book of denunciations and threats looks forward to the consummation of history and God's dealing with the sin of the world.

        2. <u>God's Love</u>

        The book is filled with sadness and sorrow, but ends in singing as God will keep His promise in delivering and blessing the remnant.

JOGGING RECORD SHEET
(Zephaniah)

THE DAY OF THE LORD'S WRATH
I. Judgment on Judah, Chapters 1:1 - 2:3
II. Judgment on Surrounding Nations, Chapters 2:4 - 3:8
III. The Future Restoration of Israel, Chapter 3:9 - 20

THE DAY OF THE LORD'S JOY
1.
2.
3.

JOGGING THROUGH HAGGAI - *Building*

"Haggai, Zechariah, and Malachi are the prophets of the return and restoration (about 538 - 432 B.C.). Persia is in power."

I. **FACTS TO KNOW**

   A. <u>WRITER</u>: Haggai, a prophet who returned with Zerubbabel from the Babylonian captivity.

   B. <u>DATE</u>: About 520 B.C.

   C. <u>KEY VERSES</u>: Haggai 1:14; 2:9

   D. <u>PURPOSE</u>: To challenge the people to return to the great project of rebuilding the temple.

   E. <u>THEME</u>: Obedience to God

II. **FOOD TO GROW**

   A. <u>HAGGAI TELLS ABOUT</u>:

   1. <u>The Rebuilding of the Temple</u>

      The people had stopped work on the temple, after facing local opposition, during their first year back home. Swayed by the preaching of Haggai and Zechariah, the work was started again in 520 B.C. and finished in 516 B.C.

   2. <u>The Messianic Kingdom</u>

   B. <u>HAGGAI AND ZECHARIAH</u>

   1. <u>Haggai</u>

      Haggai was the older man and very strong in his preaching. It was repent, get to work, or else. He was more concerned with the present and rebuilding the temple.

   2. <u>Zechariah</u>

      Zechariah was the younger man and full of vision and enthusiasm. His was a message of encouragement and gave the people a reason to work. He was more concerned with the future and building of a nation.

JOGGING RECORD SHEET
(Haggai)

I. The Exhortation to Rebuild the Temple, Chapter 1	
II. The New Temple Described, Chapter 2:1 – 19	
III. The Messianic Kingdom, Chapter 2:20–23	
1	
2	

JOGGING THROUGH ZECHARIAH — *describing*

"Getting the people back to work on the temple of God."

I. **FACTS TO KNOW**

    A. <u>WRITER</u>: Zechariah, probably born in Babylon and returned with the first group led by Zerubbabel.

    B. <u>DATE</u>: About 520 - 518 B.C.

    C. <u>KEY VERSES</u>: Zechariah 1:14; 4:6; 14:9

    D. <u>PURPOSE</u>: To encourage the people and get them back to work on building the temple.

    E. <u>THEME</u>: The future comings of Jesus Christ.

II. **FOOD TO GROW**

    A. <u>ZECHARIAH TELLS ABOUT</u>:

        1. The Rebuilding of the Temple

        2. The Future of Israel

        3. The First and Second Coming of Christ

    B. <u>ZECHARIAH SHOWS</u>:

        1. That God Remembers and Blesses in the Appointed Time

        2. That Obedience Is Better than Fasting

JOGGING NOTES

JOGGING RECORD SHEET
(Zechariah)

GOD REMEMBERS AND BLESSES IN THE APPOINTED TIME

  I. The Future of Israel, Chapters 1 - 8
 II. The First Coming of Christ, Chapters 9 - 11
III. The Second Coming of Christ, Chapters 12 - 14

OBEDIENCE IS BETTER THAN FASTING

1		8		
2		9		
3		10		
4		11		
5		12		
6		13		
7		14		

JOGGING THROUGH MALACHI — *arguing*

JOGGING NOTES

"Malachi closes the Old Testament and points to the forerunner of Christ in the New Testament. Between the Testaments we have 400 silent years."

I. **FACTS TO KNOW**

    A. <u>WRITER</u>: Malachi, a prophet of the restored Jewish nation.

    B. <u>KEY VERSES</u>: Malachi 3:9; 3:16-17

    C. <u>DATE</u>: Probably about 420 - 430 B.C., some 100 years after the Jews returned to Jerusalem.

    D. <u>THEME</u>: God rebukes sin, but promises deliverance and blessing on the basis of obedience.

    E. <u>PURPOSE</u>: To rebuke and call to repentance the people of God.

II. **FOOD TO GROW**

    A. <u>MALACHI TELLS ABOUT</u>:

        1. <u>The Sins of the People</u>

            After Nehemiah's return to Babylon, the people became discouraged and began to doubt and argue with God. They neglected worship, disobeyed God's laws and forgot His covenant. The priests were guilty of indifference and hypocrisy.

        2. <u>The Coming of Elijah</u>

            Malachi predicts the coming of Elijah which was only partially fulfilled in John the Baptist.

    B. <u>MALACHI IS UNIQUE</u>

        1. <u>It Is Written in Prose and Takes the Form of Questions and Answers.</u>

        2. <u>The People Argue With God and God Responds Through His Prophet.</u>

JOGGING RECORD SHEET
(Malachi)

THE UNGODLY SHALL BE DESTROYED
I. The Sins of the Priests, Chapters 1:1 - 2:9   II. The Sins of the People, Chapters 2:10 - 3:15   III. The Coming "Day of the Lord," Chapters 3:16 - 4:6
THE RIGHTEOUS SHALL BE SAVED
1.
2.
3.
4.

400 yrs. between Malachi & Matthew

1. History
2. Josephus
3. Apocryphal writing

Septuagint 70 scholars (285 B.C.) translate Hebrew Bible into Greek

2 Religious Parties
Sadducees & Pharisees
(liberal)   (conservatives)

63 B.C. new Power — Rome

JOGGABLE EIGHT
LET'S REVIEW

BOOK	KEY WORD	KEY PHRASE
BOOKS OF LAW		
NESIS	"BEGINNING"	BEGINNING OF THE PEOPLE OF GOD
ODUS	"LEAVING"	LEAVING EGYPT AND RECEIVING THE LAW
VITICUS	"LEARNING"	LEARNING HOW TO WORSHIP GOD
MBERS	"WANDERING"	WANDERING IN THE WILDERNESS
UTERONOMY	"REVIEWING"	REVIEWING GOD'S LAW
CONQUEST OF CANAAN		
HUA	"CONQUERING"	CONQUERING THE LAND OF CANAAN
GES	"JUDGING"	JUDGING THE SINS OF THE PEOPLE
TH	"LOVING"	LOVING THE TRUE GOD OF ISRAEL
KINGS AND KINGDOMS		
MUEL (I & II)	"REIGNING"	REIGNING AS KING OVER ISRAEL
GS (I & II)	"COLLAPSING"	COLLAPSING OF THE KINGDOM
RONICLES (I & II)	"REMEMBERING"	REMEMBERING FROM ADAM TO CAPTIVITY
RETURN AND RESTORATION		
RA	"RETURNING"	RETURNING TO JERUSALEM
HEMIAH	"REBUILDING"	REBUILDING THE WALLS
HER	"REMAINING"	REMAINING IN BABYLON

JOGGABLE EIGHT

POETRY		
JOB	"SUFFERING"	SUFFERING ALONG THE WAY
PSALMS	"SINGING"	SINGING PRAISES TO GOD
PROVERBS	"THINKING"	THINKING WISE THOUGHTS
ECCLESIASTES	"PREACHING"	PREACHING THE VANITY OF LIFE
SONG OF SOLOMON	"DELIGHTING"	DELIGHTING IN WEDDED LOVE
PROPHETS		
ISAIAH	"SAVING"	SAVING THROUGH JUDGMENT AND GRACE
JEREMIAH	"WEEPING"	WEEPING OVER JUDGMENT
LAMENTATIONS	"LAMENTING"	LAMENTING OVER JUDAH'S SINS
EZEKIEL	"UNFAILING"	UNFAILING PROMISES OF GOD
DANIEL	"INTERPRETING"	INTERPRETING THE THINGS OF GOD
HOSEA	"WOOING"	WOOING OF TRUE LOVE
JOEL	"REPENTING"	REPENTING BEFORE IT'S TOO LATE
AMOS	"DENOUNCING"	DENOUNCING INJUSTICE
OBADIAH	"REFUSING"	REFUSING PASSAGE TO ISRAEL
JONAH	"RUNNING"	RUNNING FROM GOD
MICAH	"PREDICTING"	PREDICTING A COMING JUDGMENT
NAHUM	"PRONOUNCING"	PRONOUNCING THE DESTRUCTION OF NINEVAH
HABAKKUK	"COMPLAINING"	COMPLAINING ABOUT GOD'S SLOWNESS TO ACT
ZEPHANIAH	"COMING"	COMING DAY OF GOD'S WRATH
HAGGAI	"BUILDING"	BUILDING THE TEMPLE
ZECHARIAH	"DESCRIBING"	DESCRIBING ISRAEL'S GLORIOUS FUTURE
MALACHI	"ARGUING"	ARGUING WITH GOD OVER SIN

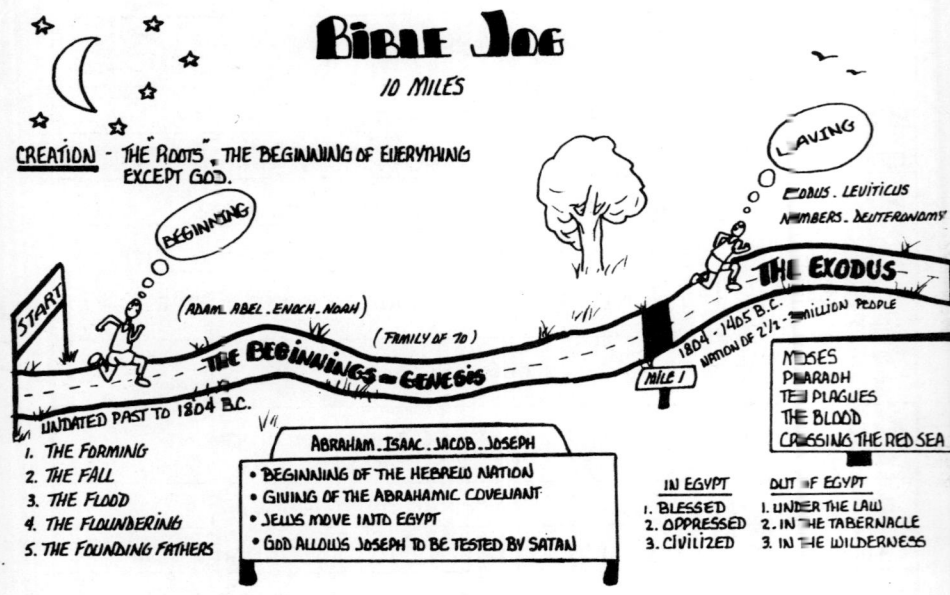

MILE ONE: The Beginnings   "Beginning"

In Genesis we find the beginning of everything except God. It is the foundation book of the Bible. The first eleven chapters contain the accounts of the creation, the temptation, the fall of man, the flood, and the Tower of Babel. The remaining chapters of Genesis tell the story of Abraham and his descendants – Isaac, Jacob, and Joseph. God begins a new era with Abraham and establishes him as the father of all believers. He entered into a covenant relationship with Abraham to give him and his seed the Land of Promise forever.

MILE TWO: The Exodus   "Leaving"

Jacob's family of some 70 people had found refuge in Egypt from the severe famine in their own land. This was made possible by Joseph, the favorite son who had been sold into slavery by his jealous brothers. Under the protection of Joseph, the family of Jacob grew into a nation of between two and three million people. Largely due to their success and size, the nation became enslaved and oppressed by Egypt, who felt threatened by their presence in their land. God called Moses, a type of Christ, to be the deliverer, leader, and lawgiver of Israel. Moses was able to lead the people of God out of Egypt and to the borders of the Promised Land.

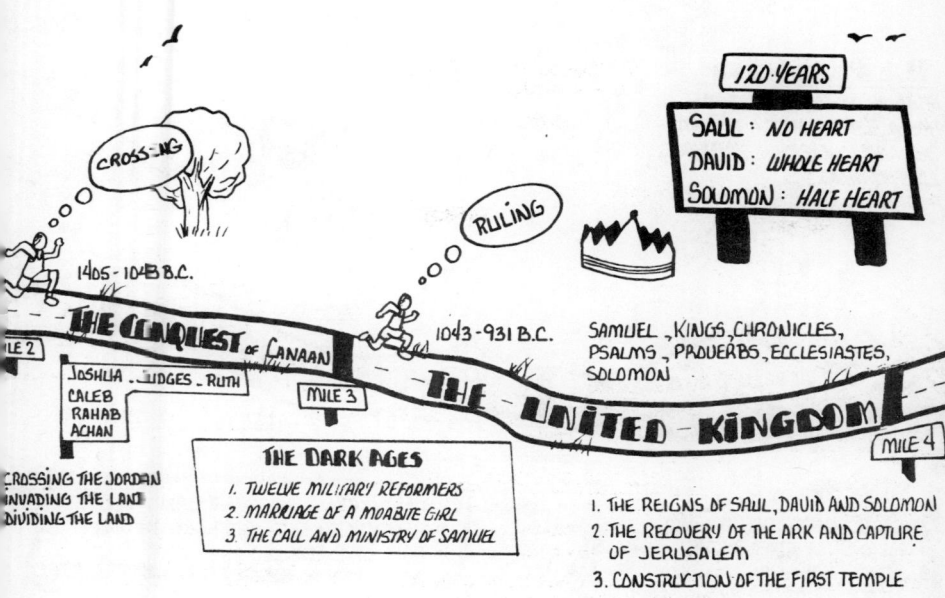

MILE THREE: The Conquest of Canaan   "Crossing"

    It was Joshua, Moses' successor, who led the people of God across the Jordan and into the Land of Promise. Following the death of Joshua, a leaderless people began to do their own thing in what is known as the "dark ages" in Israel's history. God raised up military leaders, known as judges to deliver His people from their enemies.

MILE FOUR: The United Kingdom   "Ruling"

    The people demanded a king so Samuel led them in a transition from pure theocracy to a constitutional monarchy. Saul, David and Solomon were the earthly kings to reign 40 years each over a united kingdom. This period is known as the "golden age" of Israel's history.

| MILE FIVE: | The Divided Kingdom | "Fighting" |

King Solomon left a heavy tax burden and his son Rehoboam refused to make it lighter. The northern tribes revolted and Jeroboam became king of the rival kingdom. These two kingdoms, usually in opposition, existed side by side for 259 years.

| MILE SIX: | The Captivity | "Holding" |

Judah fell, the Temple was destroyed, Jerusalem was laid in ruins, and the people of God were led away in chains. Once captive, they were treated more like colonists than slaves. One benefit of the captivity was to cure the people of idolatry.

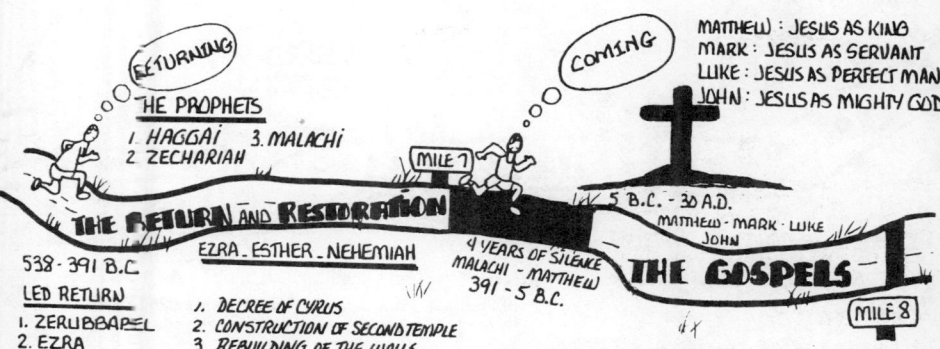

MILE SEVEN: The Return and Restoration "Returning"

God's promises and purposes were not to fail. Cyrus, king of Persia, issued a decree permitting the people to return and to rebuild the city of Jerusalem and the Temple of their God. Zerubbabel led the first group, about 50,000, back and work was begun on the Temple. In the face of opposition, work stopped on the building for 14 years and God used Haggai and Zechariah to stir up the people and get them back to work. Ezra led the second group back and instituted many important reforms among the people. Nehemiah led the third group back to Jerusalem to rebuild the walls of the city. The prophet Malachi was probably contemporary with Nehemiah.

MILE EIGHT: The Gospels "Coming"

After 400 years of silence between Malachi and Matthew, we have – in the fulness of time – the coming of Jesus into the world. Basically, all we know about Jesus we read in the gospels. The gospels record the birth, life, death, resurrection, and ascension of Christ.

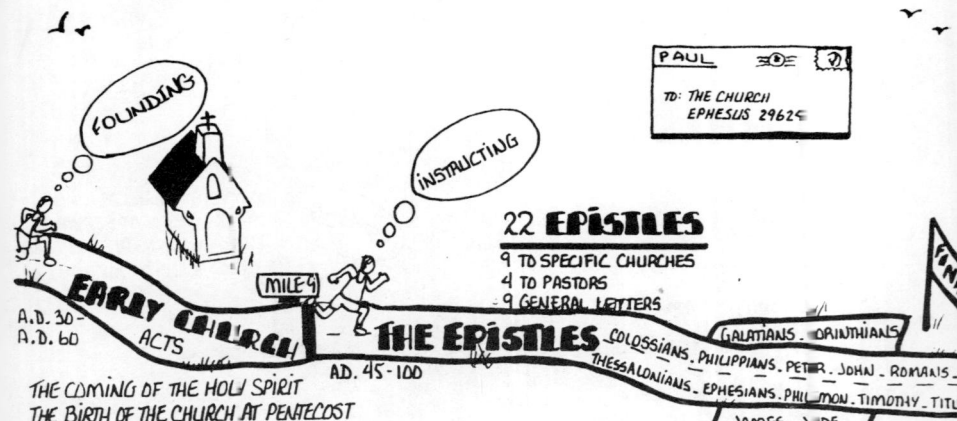

MILE NINE: The Early Church   "Founding"

Acts, the only book of history in the New Testament, records the coming of the Holy Spirit and the birth of the church at Pentecost. We learn how the church came to find itself, to know itself, and to expand itself.

MILE TEN: The Epistles   "Instructing"

Here, we find 22 letters (epistles) written to churches and to certain individuals with instructions concerning the Christian life.

Jogging Through The New Testament

Introducing The New Testament

- **Books:** 27
- **Writers:** 8
- **Time Span:** 50 Years
- **Key Words:** Faith, Hope, Love
- **Key Writers:** Peter, Apostle of Hope
  Paul, Apostle of Faith
  John, Apostle of Love

- **Subject:** Jesus
- **Theme:** Salvation
- **Dominant Idea:** Fulfilment
  Old Testament - He Is Coming
  New Testament - He Is Here

- **Central Doctrine:** Grace

The Central Theme of the New Testament

| The Founder of the Faith | Consummation of the Faith | Progress of the Faith | Subject of the Faith | Theology of the Faith |

GRACE

| Gospels | Revelation | Acts | Christ | Epistles |

| Presenting the Gospel | Revealing the Future | Spreading the Gospel | Making the Gospel Possible | Explaining the Gospel |

> For it is by His grace you are saved - through trusting Him: it is not your own doing. It is God's gift - not a reward for work done. There is nothing for for anyone to boast of. For we are God's handiwork - created in Christ Jesus to devote ourselves to the good deeds for which God has designed us.
>
> Ephesians 2:8-10 (N.E.B.)

JOGGABLE NINE

LET'S JOG THROUGH THE NEW TESTAMENT BOOKS

BOOKS OF THE NEW TESTAMENT	GOSPELS	HISTORY	LETTERS (22)		
2 7 4		**- 1**	**9**	**4**	**9**

			CHURCHES	PASTORS	GENERAL
	MATTHEW	ACTS	ROMANS	I TIMOTHY	HEBREWS
	MARK		I COR.	II TIM.	JAMES
	LUKE		II COR.	TITUS	I PETER
	JOHN		GAL.	* PHILEMON	II PETER
			* EPH.		I JOHN
			* PHIL.		II JOHN
			* COL.		III JOHN
			I THESS.		JUDE
			II THESS.		** REV.

Ephesians, Philippians, Colossians, and Philemon were written while Paul was in prison and are often referred to as "prison epistles."

Revelation, while <u>prophetic</u> for the most part, is also classified as a general letter.

JOGGABLE NINE

New Testament Authors

name	description	books written	
Matthew (JEW)	Apostle of Jesus Christ Tax Collector	Gospel of Matthew	
Mark (JEW/ROMAN)	Disciple of Apostle Peter Foreign Missionary (Servant)	Gospel of Mark	
Luke (GREEK)	Disciple of Apostle Paul Physician/Scientist	Gospel of Luke Acts of the Apostles	
John (JEW)	Apostle of Jesus Christ Fisherman	Gospel of John 1,2,3 John Revelation	
Paul (JEW)	Apostle of Jesus Christ Pharisee/Tentmaker	Romans 1,2 Cor. Galatians Ephesians Philippians	Colossians 1,2 Thess. 1,2 Timothy Titus Philemon (Hebrews?)
James (JEW)	Brother of Jesus Christ Carpenter?	James	
Peter (JEW)	Apostle of Jesus Christ Fisherman	1,2 Peter	
Jude (JEW)	Brother of Jesus Christ Carpenter?	Jude	

©1979, Educational Evangelism, Inc. Used by Permission

A BRIEF LOOK AT THE LIFE OF CHRIST
From His Birth (5 B.C.) to His Ascension (A.D. 30)

I. **THE FULNESS OF TIME** (Galatians 4:4)

   A. The world was not ready for the advent of God's Son, the Messiah. God had worked through the Greeks, Romans, and the Jews to get the world ready. Three main events led to the rapid spread of Christianity.

   1. The conquest of the world by Alexander the Great and the spread of the Greek language. God could now communicate His truth through the language of the people.

   3. The Hebrews provided a monotheistic faith as a foundation for the Gospel. And later, the scattering of the Christians through persecution caused Christianity to spread like fire throughout the known world.

II. **THE BIRTH OF JESUS**

   A. Born in Bethlehem (4 or 5 B.C.) and grew up in Nazareth.

   B. Jesus had four brothers -- James, Joses, Judas, Simon, and at least one sister (Matthew 13:55-56).

III. **THE SILENT PERIOD**

   A. The Bible gives us only glimpses of Jesus during the first two or three years of His life. From that time until about age 30 a curtain of silence falls on the life of Jesus. Only once is this silence broken and that is during a single incident at the age of 12 when Jesus visits the Temple. Then we have 18 more years of discipline, toil, and waiting for His time.

IV. **THE BEGINNING OF MINISTRY**

   A. At age 30, Jesus was baptized in the Jordan River by John the Baptist and there began His ministry.

   B. The records of the first year of ministry are scant and only given to us in John's account (the others begin with the Galilean ministry).

   C. This first year was for the most part spent in Judea and included the following:

   1. His testing in the wilderness
   2. His first disciples
   3. His first miracle (wedding in Cana).

V. THE GREAT GALILEAN MINISTRY (Second Year)

    A. Following the first year of comparative obscurity, Jesus began His more public ministry in Galilee. During the next 18 months (A.D. 27 - A.D. Jesus' ministry was characterized by growing popularity as the fame of His miracles and teachings had spread throughout the region.

        1. Performs miracles and teaches the growing crowds

        2. Calls His 12 apostles

            a. Simon Peter   g. Matthew
            b. James   h. Thomas
            c. John   i. James, son of Alphaeus
            d. Andrew   j. Thaddaeus
            e. Philip   k. Simon the Zealot
            f. Bartholomew (Nathaniel)   l. Judas Iscariot

        3. Delivers the Sermon on the Mount

        4. Makes at least three preaching tours of Galilee

        5. Popularity begans to wane

VI. THE MINISTRY IN WITHDRAWALS

    A. Lasted about three months

    B. Region around Galilee

VII. THE LATER JUDEAN MINISTRY

    A. Lasted about three months

    B. In Jerusalem and Judea

VII. THE PEREAN MINISTRY

    A. Winter and early spring

    B. On the way to Jerusalem for crucifixion

IX. THE LAST WEEK: CONDEMNATION AND DEATH

    A. Spent in Jerusalem, at time of Passover Feast

    B. His trials and death came on Thursday and Friday

X. HIS RESURRECTION

    A. Took place early Sunday morning

    B. Ascension occurred 40 days later

THE GOSPELS

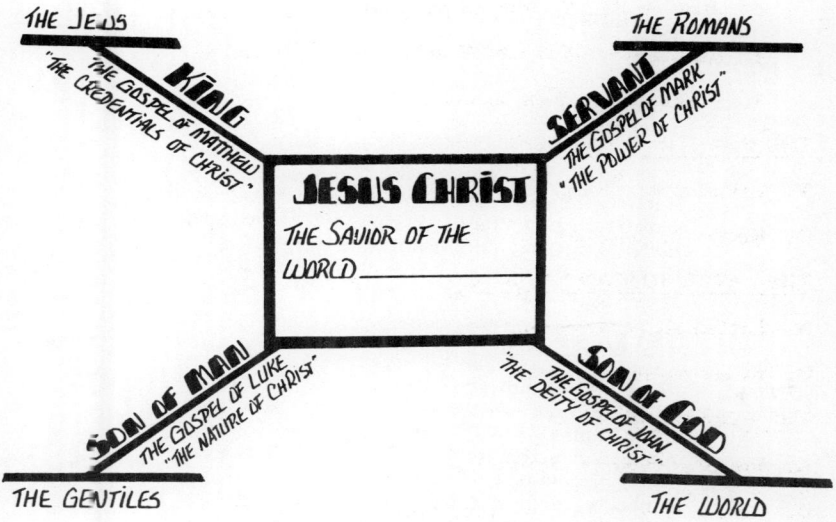

JOGGING THROUGH MATTHEW

(Jesus as King)

JOGGING NOTES: written probably 20-40 yrs after death of Jesus.

I. **FACTS TO KNOW**

  A. **WRITER**: Matthew — Writes to Jews.

  B. **DATE**: Uncertain, possibly between A.D. 50 and A.D. 70

  C. **KEY VERSES**: Matthew 1:1; 2:2; 23:27-39

  D. **KEY WORD**: Kingdom

  E. **PURPOSE**: To show that the Lord of the Christians is the Messiah of the Jews

  F. **THEME**: Portrays Jesus as the true Messiah who fulfilled the promises of the Old Testament

II. **FOOD TO GROW**

  A. **MATTHEW TELLS ABOUT**:

   1. The King (1-4)

      Matthew shows Jesus as the Messiah descending from the royal line of David. He records the birth, baptism, and temptation. The first disciples are called and Jesus begins His teaching ministry, accompanied by miracles.

   2. The Kingdom (5-16)

      Jesus sets forth the principles of the kingdom in the Sermon on the Mount -- not simply a set of rules, but the prospect of an inner change of attitude and outlook. The power of the kingdom is evidenced by some 12 miracles performed by Christ. He continued to teach, using parables, to describe the spiritual "kingdom of heaven." His miracles and teaching about the kingdom brought immediate opposition and ultimate rejection of the kingdom.

   3. The Rejection of the King (16-27)

      Matthew records the final events in the life of Christ leading up to the cross. The last week of the King on earth is described along with the events surrounding His trial, death, and burial.

4. **The Resurrected King** (22)

   Matthew does not leave Christ in a dark grave, but gives us the account of an empty tomb and a risen Lord.

B. **MATTHEW AND LUKE GIVE THE GENEALOGY OF CHRIST**

   Both Matthew and Luke give us the genealogy of Christ, but from a different perspective. Matthew ends in Joseph and shows Christ as the Son of David -- the royal line. Luke ends in Mary, giving us the legal line. Matthew writes from a Jewish perspective and Luke from a Gentile one.

JOGGING NOTES

JOGGING RECORD SHEET
(Matthew)

BEHOLD YOUR KING

A. The <u>Preparation</u> of the King, Chapters 1-4 → *Preparation*
B. The Preaching of the <u>Kingdom</u>, Chapters 5-16:12
C. The Personal Rejection of the King, Chapters 16:13 - 27:66
D. The Power of the King, Chapter 28

"WHAT SHALL I DO THEN WITH JESUS WHICH IS CALLED CHRIST" (27:22)

#		#		
1		15		
2		16		
3		17		
4		18		
5		19		
6		20		
7		21		
8		22		
9		23		
10		24		
11		25		
12		26		
13		27		
14		28		

JOGGING THROUGH MARK
(Jesus as Servant)

JOGGING NOTES

I. **FACTS TO KNOW**

   A. WRITER: Mark (John Mark)

   B. DATE: About A.D. 55-65, possibly the earliest gospel.

   C. KEY VERSES: Mark 1:1; 10:45

   D. KEY WORD: Straightway

   E. PURPOSE: To allow the wonderful work of Jesus testify to His deity and thereby convince the practical Roman mind.

   F. THEME: Jesus Christ is presented as the suffering servant who gives His life in service for others and in sacrifice for all.

II. **FOOD TO GROW**

   A. MARK TELLS ABOUT:

   1. The Servant Preparing (1:1-13)

      Mark does not give us a genealogy of Christ or anything about His birth or childhood. Rather, he emphasizes His ministry and begins with His baptism and temptation.

   2. The Servant Working (1:14 - 9:50)

      Mark presents the power of Christ and His ability to control every realm of life, including the spirit world. His emphasis on the works of Christ was to appeal to the energetic and practical Roman mindset. The Romans were a busy people who believe in power and action.

   3. The Servant Suffering (10-14)

      Mark discusses the final journey of Christ to Jerusalem and His final ministry there. He gives an account of Christ's final hours with His disciples, including the Last Supper and Gethsemane.

   4. The Servant Dying (14-15)

   5. The Servant Living Again (16:1-14)

6. **The Servant Ascending** (16:15-20)

B. MARK IS CHRONOLOGICAL AND GRAPHIC

Mark tells the story of Christ in the order things happened -- moving quickly from His baptism to the cross and resurrection. Only four paragraphs are unique to Mark. Though Mark is the shortest of the gospels, it is the most graphic and realistic account we have of the life and ministry of Jesus. He is intense and personal in portraying our Lord.

JOGGING NOTES

<u>JOGGING RECORD SHEET</u>
(Mark)

"FOR THE SON OF MAN CAME . . ."		
A. The Servant Preparing (1:1-13) B. The Servant Working (1:14 - 9:50) C. The Servant Suffering (10:1 - 14:42) D. The Servant Dying (14:43 - 15:47) E. The Servant Living - - Again (16:1-20)		
"...TO MINISTER AND TO GIVE HIS LIFE A RANSOM FOR MANY"		
1	9	
2	10	
3	11	
4	12	
5	13	
6	14	
7	15	
8	16	

JOGGING THROUGH LUKE
(Jesus as the Perfect Man)

JOGGING NOTES

I. **FACTS TO KNOW**

   A. **WRITER:** Luke, the beloved physician, and traveling companion of Paul.

   B. **DATE:** About A.C. 58 - 63

   C. **KEY VERSES:** Luke 1:4; 19:10

   D. **KEY WORD:** Compassion

   E. **PURPOSE:** To present "the Son of Man" coming to seek and save the lost.

   F. **THEME:** Jesus Christ is presented as the perfect man and the universal Saviour.

II. **FOOD TO GROW**

   A. **LUKE TELLS ABOUT**

     1. The Coming of the Perfect Man (1-2)

       Luke, the doctor, gives us the most complete and scientific biography of Christ and he does so with detailed accuracy. Luke makes clear the virgin birth and emphasizes the humanity of Christ.

     2. The Preparation of the Perfect Man (3-4)

       The genealogy of Christ in the gospel of Luke is traced in reverse order from the gospel of Matthew and goes back beyond Abraham to Adam. Luke gives the births and backgrounds of John and Jesus.

     3. The Triumph of the Perfect Man (20-24)

       In addition to the account of our Lord's death and resurrection, Luke gives us the very human account of Jesus' walk to Emmaus, after His resurrection, thereby proving the resurrection of the body and the humanity of Jesus following His resurrection.

   B. **LUKE'S STYLE**

     Luke gives an accurate and orderly account of the life of Christ. His is the most beautiful Greek in the New Testament and shows the highest touches of culture. Some have called it "the most beautiful book in the world."

JOGGING RECORD SHEET
(Luke)

> "For The Son Of Man Is Come To Seek And To Save That Which Was Lost"
>
>   A. Introduction (1:1-4)
> B. The Coming of the Perfect Man (1:5-2:52)
> C. The Preparation of the Perfect Man (3:1-4:13)
> D. The Ministry of the Perfect Man (4:14-19:28)
> E. The Triumph of the Perfect Man (19:29-24:53)

FOR ALL NATIONS AND ALL CLASSES, JESUS IS THE UNIVERSAL SAVIOUR

#		#		#	
1		13			
2		14			
3		15			
4		16			
5		17			
6		18			
7		19			
8		20			
9		21			
10		22			
11		23			
12		24			

JOGGING THROUGH JOHN
(Jesus, Eternal Son of God)

I. FACTS TO KNOW

   A. **WRITER**: John, the son of Zebedee, and the youngest of the 12 apostles.

   B. **DATE**: Uncertain, probably late, about 80-95 A.D.

   C. **KEY VERSES**: John 1:12; 3:16; 20:30-31

   D. **KEY WORD**: Believe

   E. **PURPOSE**: To establish the deity of Christ and to inspire faith in Him as the Son of God.

   F. **THEME**: The person and work of Jesus Christ.

II. FOOD TO GROW

   A. **JOHN TELLS ABOUT**:

     1. The Presentation of the Son of God (1)

       John's gospel was written much later than the other three and for a different purpose. Christianity was spreading across the empire, but its central truth of the deity of Christ was bitterly attacked. John writes to emphasize that Jesus was the eternal, incarnate Word of God. The divine presence of God who dwelt among the tribes of Israel has now come to earth in a human life.

     2. The Public Ministry of the Son of God (2-12)

       The synoptics present the facts and leave the result up to the reader, but John aims for a verdict. It is the meaning behind those facts that so concerns John. He gives meaning to events and lays stress on the spiritual. In the synoptics we learn what Jesus did and said, but John helps us interpret who He really is!

     3. The Private Ministry of the Son of God (13-17)

     4. The Passion of the Son of God (18-21)

   B. **SIGNS AND DISCOURSES**

     What the synoptics describe as miracles or mighty acts, John calls "signs", for the eye of faith goes

---

JOGGING NOTES

7 great "I am" in book of John

Bread of Life

Light of the world

The door

The good Shepherd

Resurrection + Life

The way, truth, light

True vine

JOGGING NOTES

beyond the outward act and discerns what it signified -- that Jesus was God.

C. A PARADOX

The Gospel of John is the simplest and most profound book in the New Testament. Someone has said, "in it a child can wade or an elephant can swim."

JOGGING RECORD SHEET

(John)

BUT THESE ARE WRITTEN, THAT YE MIGHT BELIEVE THAT JESUS IS THE CHRIST, THE SON OF GOD;		
<div>A. The Presentation of the Son of God (1:1-18) B. The Public Ministry of the Son of God (1:19-12:50) C. The Private Ministry of the Son of God (13:1-17:26) D. The Passion Ministry of the Son of God (18:1-21:25)</div>		
AND THAT BELIEVING YE MIGHT HAVE LIFE THROUGH HIS NAME. JOHN 20:31		
1	12	
2	13	
3	14	
4	15	
5	16	
6	17	
7	18	
8	19	
9	20	
10	21	
11		

JOGGING THROUGH ACTS

I. **FACTS TO KNOW**

    A. <u>TITLE</u>: The Greek title is "praxeis apostoin," <u>Acts of the Apostles</u>. A better title would be <u>Some Acts of the Holy Spirit</u>.

    B. <u>WRITER</u>: Luke, a Gentile physician (Col. 4:14)

    C. <u>DATE</u>: Probably about 63 A.D.

    D. <u>KEY VERSE</u>: Acts 1:8

    E. <u>KEY WORDS</u>: Spirit (54 times), Jesus (33 times), Witness (30 times)

    F. <u>THEME</u>: The resurrected, living, and empowering Christ.

    G. <u>PURPOSE</u>: To show how the work Jesus "began to do" as recorded in the gospels, was, and is continued by Him (after His ascension) through the Holy Spirit.

II. **FOOD TO GROW**

    A. <u>ACTS TELLS ABOUT</u>:

        1. <u>The Coming of the Spirit</u>

            In the first chapter we have the promise of the Spirit's coming and the second chapter records His actual coming into the world.

        2. <u>The Creation of the Church</u>

            Acts records the story of the beginning, organization, and growth of the early Christian church. It shows how the church met opposition from without and how it dealt with discipline from within.

        3. <u>The Command to Witness</u>

            In obedience to the command of Christ, Acts tells how the apostles took the gospel to all parts of the then-known world. These men of God began immediately after Pentecost, working from Jerusalem through Samaria and Galilee to Antioch. From there they went westward into many of the cities of the Roman Empire.

JOGGING NOTES

B. MAIN CHARACTERS | JOGGING NOTES

   1. Peter

      The early chapters deal mostly with the work of Peter and records his famous sermon at Pentecost.

   2. Paul

      Chapter nine records the conversion experience and baptism of Paul. The remaining chapters deal with the life and missionary journeys of Paul and his helpers.

JOGGING RECORD SHEET
(Acts)

"AND YE SHALL BE WITNESSES..."

   I.   In Jerusalem (2:1-8:3)
   II.   In Judea (8:4-12:25)
   III.   Unto Uttermost Parts of Earth (13:1-28:31)

THE CHURCH FOUNDED AND FLOURISHING

#		#	
1		15	
2		16	
3		17	
4		18	
5		19	
6		20	
7		21	
8		22	
9		23	
10		24	
11		25	
12		26	
13		27	
14		28	

JOGGING THROUGH ROMANS

JOGGING NOTES

I. **FACTS TO KNOW**

   A. <u>WRITER</u>: Paul (1:1)

   B. <u>DATE</u>: Probably written in early 58 A.D. or even 57 A.D., during Paul's third missionary journey.

   C. <u>THEME</u>: God's provision of righteousness (salvation) in Jesus Christ

   D. <u>PURPOSE</u>: To present a clear and full exposition of the gospel and to answer questions and objections concerning justification by faith.

   E. <u>KEY VERSES</u>: Romans 1:16-17

   F. <u>KEY WORD</u>: Righteous (66 times)

   G. <u>RELATIONSHIP TO OTHER BOOKS</u>: Romans has more Old Testament quotations than all the other epistles together. Although it was not written first, it was placed as the first epistle because it is the foundation book upon which the remaining truths of God's revelation build.

II. **FOOD TO GROW**

   A. <u>ROMANS TELLS ABOUT</u>:

   1. <u>The Problem of Sin</u> (Chapters 1:1 - 3:20)

      The necessity of salvation is based on the fact that all men are condemned. In chapter one, Paul shows the rejection and base immorality of the Gentiles, and they stand condemned. In chapter two, he shows that the Jews are just as guilty as the Gentiles and also stand condemned. Then, in the first 20 verses of chapter three, Paul presents the doctrine of universal condemnation for all men.

   2. <u>The Provision of Salvation</u> (Chapters 3:21 - 7:25)

      The only remedy for man is justification by faith. Justification means that God freely gives that righteousness that man can neither merit or otherwise obtain, and yet without which he must perish.

JOGGING NOTES

God's <u>grace</u> is the <u>source</u> of justification.
Christ's <u>blood</u> is the <u>ground</u> of justification.
Our <u>faith</u> is the <u>means</u> of justification.
Our <u>works</u> are the <u>evidence</u> of justification.

3. <u>The Power for Sanctification</u> (Chapter 8)

As Christ in justification delivers us from the guilt of sin, so the Holy Spirit in sanctification delivers us from the power and habits of sin. Chapter eight, where the Holy Spirit is mentioned 19 times, is a chapter showing the believer's deliverance, privileges, and assurance.

4. <u>The Purpose for the Jews</u> (Chapters 9 - 11)

Even though the Jews have rejected Christ, there is coming a time in the future when the Jews, as a nation, shall be restored to God's favor, and become a blessing to the Gentiles. God will keep His covenant with the Jews.

5. <u>The Practical Christian Life</u> (Chap. 12:1-16:27)

Out of gratitude to God for spiritual blessings in Christ, we are to yield our bodies as living, willing, and daily sacrifices to Him. Those closing chapters deal with our basic Christian responsibilities and relationships.

B. <u>ROMANS PRESENTS BOTH SIDES OF THE COIN</u>

1. The First Part of Romans Is What God Did for Us.

2. The Last Part of Romans Is What We May Do for God.

First 1/2 — What God did for us.
Last 1/2 — " We should do for God.

139

JOGGING RECORD SHEET
(Romans)

"HOW CAN SINFUL MAN GAIN A RIGHT STANDING BEFORE GOD?"

Introduction (1:1-17)
   A. Doctrinal Exposition   (1:18 - 11:36)
   B. Practical Exhortation (12:1 - 15:13)
   C. Personal Explanation (15:14 - 16:23)

"...THE JUST SHALL LIVE BY FAITH" (1:16-17)

#		#	
1		9	
2		10	
3		11	
4		12	
5		13	
6		14	
7		15	
8		16	

1. Salutation
2. Thanksgiving & Prayer
3. Doctrinal Discussion with practical application.
4. Conclusion, often with a greeting.

JOGGING THROUGH FIRST CORINTHIANS

JOGGING NOTES

I. **FACTS TO KNOW**

    A. <u>WRITER</u>: Paul (1:1) "A pastor dealing with church problems."

    B. <u>DATE</u>: Between 54 A.D. and 57 A.D., probably in the spring of 57, during third missionary journey.

    C. <u>KEY VERSE</u>: I Corinthians 13:1

    D. <u>KEY WORDS</u>: Lord, disorder

    E. <u>THEME</u>: A plea for Christian living and unity on the basis of love.

    F. <u>PURPOSE</u>: To correct the evils existing in the church, to answer their questions, and to clarify his first letter (5:9). His aim is to restore this young church, which he founded, to its former spiritual health.

II. **FOOD TO GROW**

    A. **FIRST CORINTHIANS TELLS ABOUT**:

        1. **Church Difficulties**

        This particular church had many problems such as divisions and strife, lawsuits, immorality, eating certain foods, marriage, the Lord's Supper, gifts of the Spirit, order in the church, the resurrection, and the taking of the collection.

        2. **Church Discipline**

        Because of the evidence of error and abuse, Paul presents a strong case for church discipline. He points out the need for discipline and lays down principles of discipline for the church to carry out.

        3. **Church Gifts**

        Paul takes chapters 12-14 and discusses spiritual gifts. He deals with the origin and purpose of gifts, and their proper use. The supreme gift is love.

        4. **Church Love**

        Chapter 13 is the New Testament's greatest chapter on love. In the midst of error, difficulty, and disbelief, love is to be pre-eminent.

JOGGING NOTES

5. Church Disbelief

This church had expressed disbelief concerning the fact, nature, and manner of Christ's resurrection. In chapter 15, Paul discusses the resurrection, stating the many proofs, and giving the order of events. To deny the resurrection is to make preaching, faith, and hope all in vain. In fact, no resurrection means no gospel.

JOGGING RECORD SHEET
(I Corinthians)

THE LORDSHIP OF JESUS CHRIST
Introduction (1:1-9) A. Church Divisions (1:10-4:21) B. Church Discipline (5:1-6:20) C. Church Difficulties (7:1-14:40) D. Church Disbeliefs (15:1-58) Conclusion (16:1-24)

TO CORRECT DIVISIONS AND DISORDERS WITHIN THE LOCAL CHURCH

#		#	
1	1st Letter lost	9	
2	2nd " is 1st Cor.	10	
3	3rd " " painful letter	11	
4	4th " " " 2nd Cor.	12	
5		13	
6		14	
7		15	
8		16	

JOGGING THROUGH SECOND CORINTHIANS

I. **FACTS TO KNOW**

   A. WRITER: Paul (1:1, 10:1)

   B. DATE: 56-57 A.D., about six months after First Corinthians

   C. KEY WORD: Ministry (18 times)

   D. THEME: The true gospel ministry of Jesus Christ.

   E. PURPOSE: To express gratitude for those repenting, to receive a collection for needy Christians, and to answer personal accusations.

II. **FOOD TO GROW**

   A. SECOND CORINTHIANS TELLS ABOUT:

   1. The Ministry of Paul (1:1-7:16)

   This second letter was written from Macedonia soon after Paul had left Ephesus where he almost lost his life. His first letter (First Corinthians) had been well received, but some of the church leaders were still denying that Paul was a true apostle. To validate his ministry, he tells them of his faithful preaching, the results of his ministry -- even their faith, and of his joyful suffering for the cause of the gospel. He declares his love for them and appeals for their loyalty and support.

   2. The Collection for the Christians (8:1-9:15)

   Paul makes a strong appeal for the famine-stricken Christians in Jerusalem. The Corinthians were the first to start the offering for their Jewish brothers, now they are asked to complete it that Paul's praise of them may be justified. He cites the Macedonians as an example of liberal giving in that they gave out of their poverty and beyond their power because they first gave themselves unto the Lord.

   3. The Defense of Apostleship (10:1-13:14)

   A minority of Judaizing Christians in the church accused Paul of being bold in his letters, but cowardly with them in person. He carefully defends his apostleship and promises them a third visit when he would not spare the impenitent or those who opposed the gospel. He closes by warning them not to fall back into their former sin.

JOGGING NOTES

JOGGING RECORD SHEET
(II Corinthians)

JESUS, OUR SUFFICIENCY

Introduction (1:1-11)
- A. The ministry of Paul (1:12-7:16)
- B. The Collection for the Christians (8:1-9:15)
- C. The Defense of Apostleship (10:1-13:14)

THE TRUE GOSPEL MINISTRY OF JESUS CHRIST

1		8		
2		9		
3		10		
4		11		
5		12		
6		13		
7				

JOGGABLE TEN

LET'S JOG THROUGH THE BIBLE

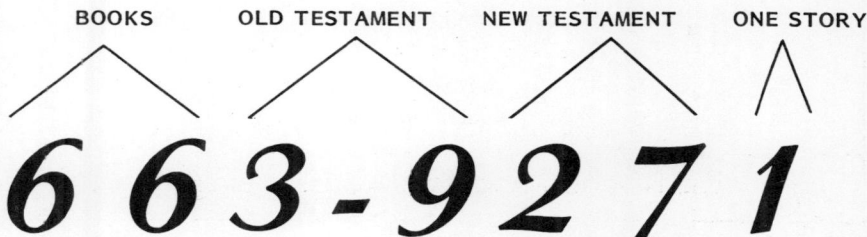

THE OLD AND NEW TESTAMENTS

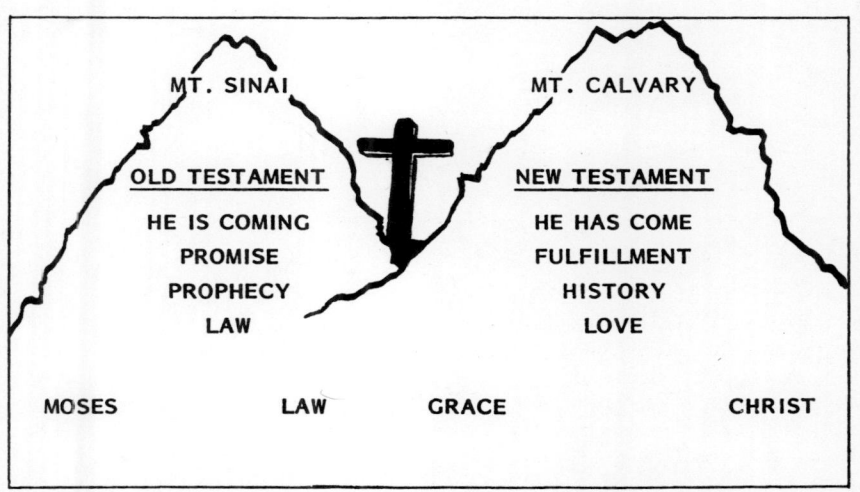

JOGGING THROUGH GALATIANS

I. **FACTS TO KNOW**

   A. <u>WRITER</u>: Paul (1:1)

   B. <u>DATE</u>: Between 48 A.D. and 56 A.D., probably about 48 A.D.

   C. <u>KEY VERSE</u>: Galatians 5:1

   D. <u>KEY WORDS</u>: Law (32 times), faith (21 times)

   E. <u>THEME</u>: Justification by faith (2:16)

   F. <u>PURPOSE</u>: To expose and condemn the false teaching of the Judaizer and to show that the believer is free from the law and saved by faith alone.

II. **FOOD TO GROW**

   A. <u>GALATIANS TELLS ABOUT</u>:

     1. <u>Paul's Gospel</u> (chapters 1-2)

     Paul was amazed that his recent converts should so quickly give up the true gospel of freedom for a Jewish message that was no gospel at all. He traces his gospel back to God Himself and says that if an angel from heaven were to preach any gospel other than that Paul preached, he would be accursed.

     2. <u>Law and Grace</u> (chapters 3-4)

     In these chapters Paul sets forth the doctrine of salvation by faith in Jesus Christ alone and His plan of salvation. In the words of Paul, "A man is not justified by <u>works</u> of the law, but through <u>faith</u> in Jesus Christ."

     3. <u>Freedom in the Spirit</u> (chapters 5-6)

     This letter to the Galatians has been called the Magna Charta of Christian liberty. It is Paul's fighting epistle and displays deep emotion and strong feeling. Freedom is in

JOGGING NOTES

the realm of the Spirit and is beyond the
legalism of the law. This is Paul's strongest
defense regarding this gospel of freedom in
Christ and is unusually severe without one
word of praise or thanksgiving. Paul is
determined to nail the <u>legalists</u> to the wall
and to prove there can be no mixture of law
and grace. He does explain how Christians
may experience this "freedom in Christ."

JOGGING
NOTES

B. KEY TO UNDERSTANDING GALATIANS

The <u>Judaizers</u>, trying to mix law and grace, were seeking to impose circumcision and the burden of the Mosaic Law on all Gentile believers as essential to their salvation. The "other gospel" Paul condemns is that of faith plus keeping the law. It will be helpful to read Acts 15 where this issue was finally debated at the Jerusalem Conference.

C. GALATIANS AND ROMANS

Someone has said that "Galatians is the sketch for the finished picture of Romans." Galatians takes up controversially what Romans puts systematically. Together, these two letters established Christianity as a world religion instead of a Jewish sect.

JOGGING RECORD SHEET
(Galatians)

"THE JUST SHALL LIVE BY FAITH"
A. Personal: The Apostle of Freedom (1-2) B. Doctrinal: The Gospel of Freedom (3-4) C. Practical: The Life of Freedom (5-6)
"TRUE FREEDOM RESULTS FROM COMPLETE ENSLAVEMENT TO CHRIST"

1	
2	
3	
4	
5	
6	

JOGGING THROUGH EPHESIANS

I. **FACTS TO KNOW**

    A. <u>WRITER</u>:   Paul (1:1)

    B. <u>DATE</u>:   Probably written in A.D. 61-62, during Paul's first imprisonment in Rome.

    C. <u>THEME</u>:   The heavenly position of the believer as a member of the body of Christ (the church) and the believer's responsibilities in Christian living as a result of his high position in Christ.

    D. <u>PURPOSE</u>:   To encourage and strengthen the believers, based upon their unique position in Christ, and to challenge them to walk worthily in their faith and calling.

    E. <u>KEY VERSES</u>:   Ephesians 1:22-23

    F. <u>KEY WORDS</u>:   In Christ (93 times)

II. **FOOD TO GROW**

    A. <u>EPHESIANS TELLS ABOUT</u>:

        1. The Believer's Blessings in Christ (1:1-3:21)

        As believers, we have been "chosen" by the Father, "redeemed" by the Son, and "sealed" by the Holy Spirit. We, who were dead in sin, have been made alive through Jesus Christ. All of this is a gift of God and is not earned by works. All men, Jew and Gentile, are united into one, reconciled by God through the giving of His Son on the cross.

        2. The Believer's Behavior in Christ (4:1-6:24)

        The book is balanced between doctrine and duty what God has done for us (chapters 1-3) and what we should do for God (chapters 4-6). Our conduct follows our calling. Paul urged the believers to practice in their daily lives all they had been taught, by putting aside their former lives of lust and corruption, assuming their new nature, created in the

JOGGING NOTES

very likeness of God. After discussing the believer's walk in Christ, he closes the book (6:10-24) with words about the believer's warfare in Christ. He encouraged them to "be strong in the Lord," to "put on the whole armor of God", and to "pray at all times."

JOGGING NOTES

B. **RELATIONSHIP TO OTHER BOOKS**

Two epistles on justification: Romans and Galatians
Two epistles on the church: Ephesians and Colossians

C. **THE CHURCH EPISTLE**

Ephesians is about the church and teaches us what the church is in the mind and heart of God and what it ought to be in practice before the eyes of the world. Ephesians emphasizes the church as the body of Christ, where Colossians emphasizes Christ as the head of the body.

JOGGING RECORD SHEET
(Ephesians)

"THE WEALTH, WALK, AND WARFARE OF THE CHRISTIAN"
A. Doctrinal: The Believer's Blessings in Christ (1-3)
B. Practical: The Believer's Behavior in Christ (4-6)
"Our Heavenly Calling in Christ Jesus"

1		
2		
3		
4		
5		
6		

JOGGING THROUGH PHILIPPIANS

JOGGING NOTES

I. **FACTS TO KNOW**

   A. <u>WRITER</u>: Paul (1:1)

   B. <u>DATE</u>: About 61-62 A.D. during Paul's first imprisonment in Rome.

   C. <u>KEY WORD</u>: Rejoice (18 times)

   D. <u>KEY VERSE</u>: Philippians 4:4

   E. <u>PURPOSE</u>: The purpose is threefold:

      1. To acknowledge receipt of a financial gift delivered by Epaphroditus

      2. To urge believers to live in <u>unity</u> with one another

      3. To send Epaphroditus home with a warm tribute to his helpfulness

   F. <u>THEME</u>: Rejoicing in the Lord regardless of circumstances.

II. **FOOD TO GROW**

   A. **PHILIPPIANS TELLS ABOUT**:

     1. <u>Christ, Our Source</u> (1:1-30)

     To Paul, Christ is life. The life that he now has originates in Christ, continues in Christ, and will one day be consummated in Christ. To live is to work for Christ, and to die is to be with Christ.

     2. <u>Christ Our Sovereign</u> (2:1-30)

     Paul uses the example of Jesus, who is God, but in submission and obedience to God His Father - gave His very life in total obedience. We are to be like Christ, but not just imitators, for we have the divine life in us. In other words, we have been energized by the Holy Spirit who enables us to think as Christ thinks, live as He lives, and love as He loves.

3. **Christ, Our Savior** (3:1-21)

    Paul warns the church of the Judaizers who insist on circumcision. He makes clear that the real circumcision are those who live a spiritual lifestyle and look to Christ alone for salvation and deliverance from sin.

4. **Christ, Our Strength** (4:1-23)

    Paul did not look at circumstances, but at Christ. He tells us to worry about nothing, pray about everything, and that will get us through anything. In all human experiences we can depend upon the strength of Christ, who makes us strong.

B. PHILIPPIANS IS A LOVE LETTER

This is Paul's sweetest letter, a love letter straight from the heart. It is a thank-you letter, a spontaneous response of love and gratitude to a generous and loving church. Remember, this joyful letter was written from inside a Roman prison where Paul was chained to a guard 24 hours a day. So, Christ is the secret of facing life.

JOGGING NOTES

JOGGING RECORD SHEET

(Philippians)

"FOR ME TO LIVE IS CHRIST AND TO DIE IS GAIN"
A. Christ is our Source (1:1-30) B. Christ is our Sovereign (2:1-30) C. Christ is our Saviour (3:1-21) D. Christ is our Strength (4:1-23)
1
2
3
4

JOGGING THROUGH COLOSSIANS

JOGGING NOTES

I. FACTS TO KNOW

    A. <u>WRITER</u>: Paul (1:1)

    B. <u>DATE</u>: Probably 61-62 A.D., near the end of Paul's first Roman imprisonment.

    C. <u>KEY VERSES</u>: Colossians 1:18-20

    D. <u>KEY WORD</u>: Head (three times)

    E. <u>PURPOSE</u>: To combat false teaching within the Colossian church and to warn those in danger of drifting away from the gospel.

    F. <u>THEME</u>: The pre-eminence of Christ as the head of the church.

II. FOOD TO GROW

    A. <u>COLOSSIANS TELLS ABOUT</u>:

        1. <u>The Fullness of God in Christ</u> (chapters 1-2)

        Paul describes Christ's seven superiorities over all other created beings. Christ is all in all (3:11) and we are complete (full) in Him. We never need to go beyond Christ for anything. <u>Christ is God's everything.</u>

        2. <u>Christian Conduct and Relationships</u> (chapter 3:4)

        Paul pleads that our old nature should be destroyed together with all it's vices, such as immorality, impurity, passion, greed, malice, slander, and unworthy talk. In their place we should put on our new garments (kindness, tenderness, humility, patience, forgiveness, and love) and live as heavenly citizens in a spiritual realm, rooted and grounded in Christ.

    B. <u>THREE DANGERS CONFRONTING ALL GENTILE CONGREGATIONS</u>

        1. <u>Astrology</u>: Planets and stars viewed as

personal gods.

2. <u>Syncretism</u>: A mixture of religions
3. <u>Gnosticism</u>: The supreme enemy of Christianity

JOGGING NOTES

JOGGING RECORD SHEET
(Colossians)

ALL THAT GOD IS, HE IS IN CHRIST – "SUPREMACY"
A. Doctrinal: "The Fullness of God is Christ" (1-2)
B. Practical: "Christian Conduct and Relationships" (3-4)
ALL THAT HE IS IN CHRIST, HE WANTS TO BE IN US – "SUFFICIENCY"

1	
2	
3	
4	

JOGGING THROUGH FIRST THESSALONIANS

I. **FACTS TO KNOW**

   A. **WRITER**: Paul (1:1)

   B. **DATE**: About 51-52 A.D., during the early part of Paul's stay in Corinth.

   C. **KEY VERSES**: 1 Thessalonians 1:9-10

   D. **KEY WORD**: Coming (four times)

   E. **PURPOSE**: Paul had to leave Thessalonica in a hurry due to the opposition to the gospel. Later, Timothy brought Paul word from the church along with questions they had raised. Paul wrote in response to their overture.

   F. **THEME**: The glorious second coming of Jesus Christ.

II. **FOOD TO GROW**

   A. **FIRST THESSALONIANS TELLS ABOUT**:

   1. **Looking Back**: "How they were saved" (1:1-3:13)

      Paul writes with thanksgiving concerning the proof of their true conversion and their manifestation of the Christian graces. He thanks God for this church because of the growth and their faith and their increasing love for one another.

   2. **Looking Around**: "How they were to live" (4:1-12)

      Paul urges the believers to abstain from all immorality, live quietly, mind their own business, and to work with their hands. The walk of the Christian is all important. A Christian is not to do as he pleases, but as it pleases Christ.

   3. **Looking Ahead**: "How they were to prepare: (4:13-5:28)

      In what is labeled as one of the most important prophetic passages in the scriptures, Paul deals with what death means to a Christian and what the rapture means to the church. Those whose loved ones have fallen asleep in death should not give way to hopeless

JOGGING NOTES

sorrow or feel that they have missed the
rapture. Rather, they are to be comforted
in the fact that at the coming of the Lord, it
is not the living who shall greet the Lord
first, but the dead shall rise from their graves
followed by those alive. As to the time of
His coming, it will be unexpected as a thief
in the night. Therefore, while others sleep,
we must be wide awake and living God-
controlled lives.

JOGGING NOTES

B. **APOSTASY**

A doctrinal departure by professing Christians
who have never really been saved and who reject
the basic truths of the Christian faith.

JOGGING RECORD SHEET

(I Thessalonians)

"THE SECOND COMING OF JESUS CHRIST"

A. LOOKING BACK: "HOW THEY WERE SAVED" (1:1-3:13)
B. LOOKING AROUND: "HOW THEY WERE TO LIVE" (4:1-12)
C. LOOKING AHEAD: "HOW THEY WERE TO PREPARE (4:13-5:28)

A COMFORTING AND INSPIRING HOPE

1	
2	
3	
4	
5	

JOGGING THROUGH SECOND THESSALONIANS

I. **FACTS TO KNOW**

   A. **WRITER**: Paul (1:1)

   B. **DATE**: Shortly after First Thessalonians, about 52-53 A.D.

   C. **PURPOSE**: To affirm the fundamentals of the faith, to condition the believers to go on in holy living, and to comfort them concerning the return of the Lord.

   D. **THEME**: The second coming of Christ.

   E. **KEY VERSE**: II Thessalonians 2:15

   F. **KEY WORD**: Coming (three times)

II. **FOOD TO GROW**

   A. **SECOND THESSALONIANS TELLS ABOUT**:

   1. **The Privilege of Suffering** (1:3-12)

   In this world the Christians will suffer and experience persecution. This is not to be confused with the "great tribulation." The Thessalonian Christians were "shaken in mind" and "troubled" by deceivers who made some believe that they were already passing through the "great tribulation" and that "the day of the Lord" was already here.

   2. **The Promise of His Coming** (2:1-17)

   Second Thessalonians tells about Christ coming with His mighty angels, and emphasizes that this coming will be a terror for the disobedient. According to Paul, Christ's coming for His church and His coming with His mighty angels are two aspects of but one occurrence.

   (a) **The First Aspect**: (I Thessalonians 4:17)

   (1) Christ will descend from heaven.
   (2) The shout of the archangel will be heard.
   (3) The dead in Christ will rise first.

                (4) All other believers will be caught up
                    with the Lord in the clouds.
                (5) At this time, He will be seen only by
                    His own.
                (6) Next, the Jews occupy their own land
                    of Palestine.
                (7) The Gentile nations gather against
                    Israel.
                (8) The Anti-Christ becomes the world-
                    ruler.
                (9) The Anti-Christ makes a covenant with
                    the Jews and breaks it.
                (10) The "great tribulation" (Matthew 23:
                    21, 22)

            (b) The Second Aspect: (Matthew 25:31)

                (1) Christ will come with His Church.
                (2) He will set up His kingdom on earth

    3. The Practice of Christian Living (3:1-18)

        The time of the glorious return of the Lord is
        left with God Himself. In the meantime, we
        are to take advantage of opportunities of
        service and to live every day in view of His
        personal return.

B. THE MAN OF SIN (The Anti-Christ)

    Immediately following the rapture of the church,
    the "lawless" one will be revealed. He will be
    worshipped as God and will rise to great power,
    and rule the world with power, signs, and lying
    wonders. His name will be Anti-Christ and when
    Christ comes back with His saints, He will
    destroy the Anti-Christ.

JOGGING NOTES

JOGGING RECORD SHEET
(II Thessalonians)

THE SECOND COMING OF JESUS CHRIST
A. The privilege of suffering (1) B. The promise of His coming (2) C. The practice of Christian living (3)
CHRISTIANS ARE TO BE WATCHING, WAITING, & WORKING UNTIL HE COMES
1.
2.
3.

JOGGING THROUGH FIRST TIMOTHY

JOGGING NOTES

I. **FACTS TO KNOW**

    A. <u>WRITER</u>: Paul (1:1)

    B. <u>DATE</u>: About 63-65 A.D.

    C. <u>PURPOSE</u>: To encourage, instruct, and exhort young pastors in charge of churches.

    D. <u>THEME</u>: Proper order, procedure, and doctrine in the church.

    E. <u>KEY VERSE</u>: I Timothy 3:15

    F. <u>KEY WORDS</u>: Doctrine (eight times), teach (seven times)

II. **FOOD TO GROW**

    A. FIRST TIMOTHY TELLS ABOUT:

        1. Church Doctrine (1:3-20)

        Paul charges Timothy not to mix fables and legends with the glorious gospel of the blessed Lord. He is to hold faith and a good conscience.

        2. Church Worship (2:1-15)

        The church members are exhorted to pray for those in authority over them as well as for all men. Guidelines of conduct at worship are given for the men and the women.

        3. Church Organization (3:1-4:5)

        Paul gives the qualifications for pastors, deacons, and their wives. He emphasizes the need for Christian behavior - especially among church leaders.

        4. Church Administration (4:6-6:21)

        Here, Paul gives specific direction for the pastor: He is to warn the church of error, to be a Christ-like example, and to develop as a minster of the gospel. Paul closes with instruction regarding various groups within the church.

JOGGING NOTES

B. THE PASTORAL EPISTLES:

First Timothy, Second Timothy, and Titus are called "Pastoral Epistles" because they deal so much with the problems and procedures of a pastor and his flock.

JOGGING RECORD SHEET
(I Timothy)

A CHURCH ORGANIZED AND FUNCTIONING
A. Church doctrine (1:1-3:20)   B. Church worship (2:1-15)   C. Church organization (3:1-4:5)   D. Church administration (4:6-6:21)
WITH SPIRITUAL LEADERSHIP

1	
2	
3	
4	
5	
6	

JOGGING THROUGH SECOND TIMOTHY

I. **FACTS TO KNOW**

    A. WRITER: Paul (1:1)

    B. DATE: About 66 - 67 A.D., after Paul is back in prison and facing imminent execution (4:6-8)

    C. PURPOSE: To give final instructions to Timothy, his son in the ministry, regarding the proper course for a true servant of God during times of persecution and apostasy.

    D. THEME: Paul's farewell words of instruction and encouragement.

    E. KEY VERSE: II Timothy 2:15

    F. KEY WORDS: Good (five times), ashamed (five times)

II. **FOOD TO GROW**

    A. SECOND TIMOTHY TELLS ABOUT:

        1. Timothy

        Paul expresses gratitude for Timothy's ministry and for his love and support. He exhorts Timothy regarding the ministry and warns him of the perils of apostasy. He charges Timothy to preach the word with consistency and courage.

        2. Paul

        This letter is Paul's last, his swan song. He gives his personal testimony as he nears the end of his course. It is the valedictory address of the greatest man, outside of Christ, who ever lived on this earth. (II Timothy 4:7-8)

        3. Others

        This is a very personal letter with references to 23 people. The very heartbeat of Paul is evident as he gives his parting words to his close friends.

JOGGING NOTES

B. **THE INSPIRATION OF SCRIPTURE:**

    Second Timothy gives us Paul's strongest statement on the inspiration of scripture and it's authority in the life of the Christian minister. (II Timothy 2:15; 3:15-17)

JOGGING NOTES

JOGGING RECORD SHEET
(II Timothy)

THE APOSTLE PAUL'S FAREWELL ADDRESS
A. Gratitude for Timothy's ministry (1:1-1:18) B. Timothy exhorted (2:1-26) C. Timothy warned (3:1-17) D. Timothy charged (4:1-22)
ABSOLUTE LOYALTY TO CHRIST, NO MATTER WHAT!
1.
2.
3.
4.

JOGGING THROUGH TITUS

I. **FACTS TO KNOW**

    A. <u>WRITER</u>: Paul (1:1)

    B. <u>DATE</u>: About 63-66 A.D., between Paul's first and second imprisonment.

    C. <u>PURPOSE</u>: To give specific qualifications for spiritual leadership and to establish the standard for godly living.

    D. <u>THEME</u>: The godly life of the believer and his relationship to the church.

    E. <u>KEY VERSE</u>: Titus 1:5

    F. <u>KEY WORD</u>: Sound (doctrine, faith, speech) seven times

II. **FOOD TO GROW**

    A. TITUS TELLS ABOUT:

        1. An Orderly Church (1:1-16)

        An orderly church must have <u>ordained</u> leaders who must meet the prescribed <u>requirements</u>. Such leaders have spiritual oversight of the churches as well as being teachers of the Word.

        2. A Sound Church (2:1-15)

        It is all important what we believe for belief determines behavior. The church is to teach and preach sound doctrine.

        3. A Practical Church (3:1-15)

        Church members should be devoted to good works, and such works are evidence of salvation. The church member is to be submissive to rulers and authorities, to speak ill of no one, to avoid quarreling, and to show a gentle spirit in dealing with others.

    B. THE STANDARD FOR THE NEW TESTAMENT CHURCH

        The book of Titus contains a basic description of the New Testament church in its organization and operation.

JOGGING NOTES

C. **THE CHRISTIAN LIFE** JOGGING NOTES

  Two of the most comprehensive statements regarding the Christian life are to be found in the book of Titus. (2:11-14; 3:4-7)

JOGGING RECORD SHEET
(Titus)

THE IDEAL CHURCH
A. An orderly church (1:1-16) B. A sound church (2:1-15) C. A practical church (3:1-15)
"AN ORDERLY ORGANIZATION, SOUND IN DOCTRINE, PURE IN LIFE, READY TO WORK"
1.
2.
3.

JOGGING THROUGH PHILEMON

JOGGING NOTES

I. FACTS TO KNOW

　A. WRITER: Paul (1:1)

　B. DATE: About 61-62 A.D.

　C. KEY VERSES: Philemon 1:17-19

　D. PURPOSE: To illustrate Christ's love for us in pleading our case before God.

　E. THEME: Forgiveness through Christ.

II. FOOD TO GROW

　A. PHILEMON TELLS ABOUT:

　　1. Philemon: Paul's friend and the master of a run-away slave (1-7)

　　2. Onesimus: A run-away slave and thief (8-17)

　　3. Paul's Promise of Payment: To cover any losses caused by Onesimus (18-25)

　B. PHILEMON IS A STORY OF FORGIVENESS.

　C. PHILEMON IS AN ILLUSTRATION OF SUBSTITUTION.

JOGGING RECORD SHEET
(Philemon)

THE LIBERATING POWER OF THE GOSPEL
A. Paul's praise for Philemon (v. 1-7)   B. Paul's plea for Onesimus (v. 8-17)   C. Paul's promise of payment (v. 18-25)
IN CHANGING A CRIMINAL INTO A CHRISTIAN BROTHER
1

JOGGING THROUGH HEBREWS

JOGGING NOTES

I. **FACTS TO KNOW**

   A. **WRITER**: Paul, though there is a great difference of opinion as to who actually wrote the book.

   B. **DATE**: Around 64-67 A.D.

   C. **KEY WORD**: Better (13 times)

   D. **KEY VERSE**: Hebrews 4:14

   E. **PURPOSE**: To prevent apostasy from Christianity back to Judaism and to comfort Christians enduring suffering and persecution.

   F. **THEME**: Presenting the priesthood of Christ along with His person and work, as being superior to that of the Levitical priests and institutions.

II. **FOOD TO GROW**

   A. **HEBREWS TELLS ABOUT**:

   1. The Superiority of Christ (1:1-10:18)

      Jesus Christ is superior to everyone and in all things. He is superior to the Old Testament prophets, the priesthood, and the angels. He is above all.

   2. The Superior Lifestyle Made Possible by Christ (10:19-13:25)

      In the first ten chapters, Paul presents his convincing argument for the superiority of Christ. The remaining three chapters are given to the application of the argument. Christ is the author of a superior lifestyle available to every Christian.

   B. **KEY TO UNDERSTANDING**

      Hebrews was written to Hebrew Christians who were undergoing such severe persecution that they were tempted to turn back. Zealous rabbis did anything short of murder to bring back Christian converts to the Jewish religion.

JOGGING RECORD SHEET
(Hebrews)

"LOOKING UNTO JESUS, THE AUTHOR AND FINISHER OF OUR FAITH" (12:2)

CHRIST IS SUPERIOR

A. THE ARGUMENT (1:1-10:18)

1. Christ is superior to the prophets (1:1-3)
2. Christ is superior to the angels (1:4-2:18)
3. Christ is superior to the Old Testament priesthood (3:1-4:13)

B. THE APPLICATION (10:19-13:25)

1. The privileges of faith (10:19-39)
2. The patriarchs of faith (11:1-40)
3. The perseverance of faith (12:1-29)
4. The practice of faith (13:1-25)

". . .ONCE OFFERED TO BEAR THE SINS OF MANY" (9:28)

#	
1	
2	
3	
4	
5	
6	
7	
8	
9	
10	
11	
12	
13	

JOGGING THROUGH JAMES

JOGGING NOTES

I. **FACTS TO KNOW**

   A. <u>WRITER</u>: James (1:1), the brother of Jesus.

   B. <u>DATE</u>: Between 40 and 55 A.D.

   C. <u>KEY VERSES</u>: James 1:22; 2:20

   D. <u>KEY WORDS</u>: Faith (16 times); works (15 times)

   E. <u>PURPOSE</u>: To encourage and exhort Christians to demonstrate their faith by their deeds.

   F. <u>THEME</u>: A holy life and good works are the results of a true profession of faith in Christ.

II. **FOOD TO GROW**

   A. <u>JAMES TELLS ABOUT</u>:

   1. <u>Suffering</u>

      Suffering builds character and also reveals character. God allows such suffering to refine us and to make us more like Himself.

   2. <u>Service</u> (2:1-26)

      According to James, a genuine faith will be expressed in love and will prove itself by works.

   3. <u>Speech</u> (3:1-18)

      James devotes an entire chapter (3:1-18) to a discussion of the power and perversity of the tongue.

   4. <u>Separation</u> (4:1-17)

      True Christian faith involves a life of separation. Therefore, the Christian must do constant battle with three basic enemies: 1) the world 2) the flesh 3) and the devil.

5. The Second Coming (5:1-20)

   James devotes the final chapter to a very practical discussion of the second coming of Christ.

B. A GUIDE TO DAILY RELIGION

   The book of James seems to be the most practical book of all the epistles. It is the Proverbs of the New Testament.

JOGGING NOTES

JOGGING RECORD SHEET
(James)

PRESENTING A PRACTICAL, WORKING FAITH
A. A practical faith and suffering (1:1-27) B. A practical faith and service (2:1-26) C. A practical faith and speech (3:1-18) D. A practical faith and separation (4:1-17)
CHRISTIANS SHOW THEIR FAITH BY THEIR WORKS

1	
2	
3	
4	
5	

JOGGING THROUGH FIRST PETER

JOGGING NOTES

I. **FACTS TO KNOW**

   A. <u>WRITER</u>: Simon Peter (1:1)

   B. <u>DATE</u>: About 63 – 65 A.D.

   C. <u>KEY VERSES</u>: I Peter 1:13; 2:9–11; 4:13

   D. <u>KEY WORD</u>: Suffering (21 times, 6 implied)

   E. <u>PURPOSE</u>: To give hope in the midst of suffering and difficult circumstances.

   F. <u>THEME</u>: Christian hope in the time of trial.

II. **FOOD TO GROW**

   A. <u>FIRST PETER TELLS ABOUT</u>:

      1. A personal salvation.

      2. A promising life.

      3. A glorious reward.

   B. <u>KEY TO UNDERSTANDING</u>

   Suffering is common to all and the Christian should not be shocked by the "fiery trials" that come. Christianity does not exempt one from pain, misforturnes, bereavement, or death. In addition, Satan will try to use suffering against us. Therefore, we are to endure suffering patiently and allow it to produce positive effects in our lives.

JOGGING RECORD SHEET
(I Peter)

GOD'S MESSAGE TO SUFFERING CHRISTIANS

- A. Greeting (1:1-2)
- B. The declaration of personal salvation (1:3-12)
- C. The challenge of a promising life (1:13-4:19a)
- D. The glorious reward that is predicted (4:19a-5:11)
- E. Conclusion (4:12-14)

HOW TO SUFFER PATIENTLY, JOYOUSLY, AND TO GOD'S GLORY!

1	
2	
3	
4	
5	

JOGGING THROUGH SECOND PETER

I. FACTS TO KNOW

    A. <u>WRITER</u>: Simon Peter (1:1)

    B. <u>DATE</u>: About 65 - 67 A.D.

    C. <u>KEY WORD</u>: Knowledge (16 times)

    D. <u>KEY VERSES</u>: II Peter 2:1; 3:18

    E. <u>PURPOSE</u>: To issue a call to a holy and godly life to be lived in view of the second coming of Christ.

    F. <u>THEME</u>: Christian growth in the grace and knowledge of the Lord Jesus Christ.

II. <u>FOOD TO GROW</u>

    A. SECOND PETER TELLS ABOUT:

        1. Christian growth

        2. False teachers

        3. The coming of Christ

    B. TRUE KNOWLEDGE

    The central theme of Second Peter is true spiritual knowledge based on a personal and growing relationship with Jesus Christ (3:18).

    C. THE INSPIRATION OF SCRIPTURES

    Peter's statement on the nature of the scriptures in 1:21 is one of the most definitive passages on inspiration to be found in the New Testament.

JOGGING NOTES

JOGGING RECORD SHEET
(II Peter)

CHRISTIAN GROWTH AND HOPE
A. True knowledge and Christian growth (Ch. 1) B. True knowledge and false teachers (Ch. 2) C. True knowledge and the coming of Christ (Ch. 3)
". . . IN THE KNOWLEDGE OF OUR LORD AND SAVIOUR JESUS CHRIST."
1
2
3

JOGGING THROUGH FIRST JOHN

I. **FACTS TO KNOW**

    A. <u>WRITER</u>:   John the apostle.

    B. <u>DATE</u>:   Between 85 and 95 A.D., probably 90 A.D.

    C. <u>PURPOSE</u>:   To help guide the Christian into a life of real joy based on the complete assurance we have in Christ.

    D. <u>THEME</u>:   Love, light, and life as revealed through Jesus Christ.

II. **FOOD TO GROW**

    A. <u>FIRST JOHN TELLS ABOUT</u>:

        1. <u>Fellowship</u> (1:1-28)

        Our God is light and walking with Him in the light means fellowship one with another.

        2. <u>Obedience</u> (2:1-4:6)

        God is righteous, therefore fellowship with Him depends on our obedience.

        3. <u>Sonship</u> (4:7-5:21)

        We are called sons through the Father's love and we are to show that love by loving one another.

    B. **THREE IMPORTANT STRANDS**

    Three strands are woven throughout the epistle:

    1. Light versus darkness

    2. Love versus hate

    3. Truth versus error

JOGGING RECORD SHEET
(I John)

FELLOWSHIP WITH GOD AND LIFE ETERNAL

A. Fellowship: God is light (1:1-28)
B. Obedience: God is righteousness (2:29-4:6)
C. Sonship: God is love (4:7-5:21)

GOD IS LOVE - GOD IS LIGHT - GOD IS LIFE

1	
2	
3	
4	
5	

JOGGING THROUGH SECOND JOHN

I. FACTS TO KNOW

    A. WRITER: John the apostle

    B. DATE: Between 85 and 95 A.D., probably 90 A.D.

    C. KEY WORDS: truth (5 times); love (4 times)

    D. KEY VERSES: II John 7, 9, and 10

    E. PURPOSE: To re-emphasize the need for walking in truth and being aware of existing error.

    F. THEME: Truth is worth standing for and living by.

II. FOOD TO GROW

    A. SECOND JOHN TELLS ABOUT:

       1. Truth

       Walking in truth means that we love one another, obey God's commands, and maintain a strong loyalty to the true doctrines of the gospel.

       2. Error

       It seems that some Christians were unknowingly entertaining some imposters and heretics. John warns that to entertain a teacher of error is to approve of his evil works and to share his guilt.

    B. A SUMMARY STATEMENT

    The Christian is to walk in truth and love.

JOGGING NOTES

JOGGING RECORD SHEET
(II John)

GOD IS TRUTH
A. Walk in truth (vv. 1-4) B. Love one another (vv. 5-6) C. Receive not deceivers (vv. 7-11) D. Respond in joyous fellowship (vv. 12-13)
WALK IN TRUTH AND LOVE

| 1 | |

JOGGING THROUGH THIRD JOHN

I. FACTS TO KNOW

   A. WRITER: John the apostle

   B. DATE: Between 85 and 95 A.D., probably around 90 A.D.

   C. KEY WORD: truth (7 times)

   D. KEY VERSES: III John 1:8, 11

   E. PURPOSE: To encourage Gaius in his Christian hospitality and to deal with Diotrephes, a self-appointed dictator.

   F. THEME: Truth is worth working for.

II. FOOD TO GROW

   A. THIRD JOHN TELLS ABOUT:

   1. Gaius, who walks in truth (1-8).

   2. Diotrephes, who opposes the truth (9-11)

   3. Demetrius, who is an example of the truth (12-14)

   B. A SUMMARY STATEMENT

   Diotrephes, a church leader who loved the pre-eminence, led a movement to exclude Gaius and his friend from the church because of their missionary generosity and hospitality. John writes this personal letter to commend Gaius and to promise to come later to deal with Diotrephes.

JOGGING NOTES

JOGGING RECORD SHEET
(III John)

THE TRUTH EXPRESSED IN LOVE

A. Gaius: Walks in the truth (1-8)
B. Diotrephes: Opposes the truth (9-11)
C. Demetrius: An example of the truth (12)
D. Conclusion (13-14)

"THINKING MORE HIGHLY OF OTHERS THAN HIMSELF" (Phil. 2:3)

1	

JOGGING THROUGH JUDE

I. **FACTS TO KNOW**

    A. <u>WRITER</u>: Jude (English form of Judas), brother of James, and a half-brother of Jesus.

    B. <u>DATE</u>: 66 - 69 A.D.

    C. <u>PURPOSE</u>: To instruct and encourage believers and to warn of false teachers (v.3).

    D. <u>THEME</u>: Christians are to "earnestly contend for the faith".

    E. <u>KEY WORD</u>: Ungodly (5 times)

II. **FOOD TO GROW**

    A. <u>JUDE TELLS ABOUT</u>:

        1. <u>Apostasy</u>

        There were false teachers who were practicing lawlessness and had perverted the true doctrines of God's grace and Christian liberty. Jude warns his readers against such teachers.

        2. <u>Sin</u>

        The book of Jude is one of the most forceful passages in the New Testament concerning the awfulness of sin.

    B. <u>JUDE AND REVELATION</u>

    Jude offers a very appropriate introduction to the book of Revelation.

JOGGING NOTES

JOGGING RECORD SHEET
(Jude)

OUR DUTY IN THE MIDST OF APOSTASY

A. Greetings (1-2)
B. Exhortation: Defense of the faith (3-4)
C. Illustration: Departures from the faith (5-16)
D. Admonition: Discipline in the faith (17-23)
E. Conclusion: Doxology (24-25)

KEEP THE FAITH

JOGGING THROUGH REVELATION

JOGGING NOTES

I. **FACTS TO KNOW**

   A. <u>WRITER</u>: John, the Apostle and beloved disciple.

   B. <u>DATE</u>: Probably around 95 A.D., during the time of great persecution.

   C. <u>KEY WORDS</u>: I saw, beheld, looked (49 times)
                         Lamb, Christ (26 times)
                         Throne (44 times)

   D. <u>KEY VERSE</u>: Revelation 1:19

   E. <u>PURPOSE</u>: To reveal Jesus Christ as redeemer, conqueror of all evil, and the only hope for the future.

   F. <u>THEME</u>: The unveiling of Jesus Christ as King of kings and Lord of lords.

II. **FOOD TO GROW**

   A. <u>REVELATION TELLS ABOUT</u>:

      1. <u>The Coming of Christ</u>

      In the very first chapter we find a specific reference to the visible return of Christ. ". . . He cometh with clouds and every eye shall see Him" (Rev. 1:7).

      2. <u>The Vision of Christ</u> (1:1-1:20)

      In chapter one (1:9-20), John gives a detailed description of the glorified Christ. He goes from His white hair down to His feet. These physical characteristics have corresponding spiritual meaning.

      3. <u>The Seven Churches</u> (2:1-3:22)

      In chapters 2 and 3 we have a message to seven different churches. These stirring messages were directed to seven specific local churches in existence at that time. However, the timeless messages are equally applicable to all churches today.

4. The Future Events   (4:1-22:21)

   Beginning with chapter 4, Revelation deals with future events - the things which shall be hereafter:

   (1) The rapture of the church (chapters 4 and 5)

   (2) The seven year tribulation (chapters 6-19)

   (3) The millennial reign of Christ (chapter 20)

   (4) The new heaven and the new earth (chapters 21 and 22)

B. A BOOK OF PROMISE AND JUDGMENT

   The promise is for those who are sealed and the judgment is for Satan and those allied with him. The satanic power must work itself out toward the consummation at the last day, but its final defeat and ultimate doom are absolutely certain. Christ is victorious and we have won!

C. KEY TO UNDERSTANDING

   Because of the abundance of symbols and imagery found in Revelation, there are many things that we still do not fully understand. Let's not get bogged down in what we don't know, but rather obey and proclaim what we do know. "Now we see through a glass darkly, but one day we shall see Him face to face" and then we shall know all things.

JOGGING NOTES

JOGGING RECORD SHEET
(Revelation)

"TO HIM WHO LOVES US. . ." (1:5)		
A. Introduction (1:1-8) B. A visitation of the glorified Christ (1:9-20) C. A message to the seven churches (2:1-3:22) D. An unveiling of the future (4:1-22:21)		
"EVEN SO, COME LORD JESUS" (22:20)		
1	12	
2	13	
3	14	
4	15	
5	16	
6	17	
7	18	
8	19	
9	20	
10	21	
11	22	